PAUL E. JOHNSON is one of the real pioneers in the field of pastoral counseling. As a professor of psychology and pastoral counseling at Boston University from 1941 to 1963, he developed programs for clinical pastoral education and served as director of the Pastoral Counseling Service there from 1952 until his retirement in 1963.

He now directs the Indianapolis Pastoral Counseling Center and is a visiting professor of pastoral counseling at Christian Theological Seminary in Indianapolis.

Dr. Johnson is a graduate of Cornell College, Mt. Vernon, Iowa (A.B.); University of Chicago (A.M.); and Boston University (S.T.B. and Ph.D.). Before joining the faculty at Boston University, he was a pastor and missionary and also taught and did guidance work at Hamline University and Morningside College.

He has written extensively for journals and magazines and is the author of *Psychology of Religion* and *Psychology of Pastoral Care*, both published by Abingdon Press.

PERSON
AND
COUNSELOR

PERSON AND COUNSELOR

Paul E. Johnson

Nashville Abingdon Press *New York*

PERSON AND COUNSELOR

Library of Congress Catalog Card Number: 67–11710

SET UP, PRINTED, AND BOUND BY THE PARTHENON PRESS, AT NASHVILLE, TENNESSEE, UNITED STATES OF AMERICA

To the persons and counselors
who have the faith and courage
to open their hearts to new
life in counseling

Foreword

Through my years of learning and teaching, I have been seeking a unifying concept to give central meaning to the experiences of human life. If we could sum up this central meaning in one word, which of course we cannot, I would spell it *response*.

The most wonderful gift of life is the ability to respond. In order to respond there must be a dynamic sustaining universe where each moving impulse is sensitive and interactive to every other event. To be a person is to respond to other persons in unique ways that are characteristic of a human community. The capacity to be a person may be inherited, but the achievement of this potentiality is the response of person to person. In creative terms, how can we say it better than these truly revealing words.

And the Lord God formed man of the dust of the ground, and breathed into his nostrils the breath of life; and man became a living soul.

So God created man in his own image, in the image of God created he him; male and female created he them. (Gen. 2:7; 1:27).

Persons are created in the image of a person by giving forth from each to each the breath of life. No one is born alone to live alone but to grow into personhood by the mediation of persons who interchange life for life. Only a person can mediate for a person in the search to fulfill his human destiny. The work of counseling is such a mediation of person for person.

When we see counseling in these terms we may call it responsive counseling. A counselor is responsive to the person by caring enough to listen, to accept, and to search profoundly with him for the meaning of his life. To be responsive in this sense calls for complete dedication and continuing preparation.

This book is concerned with the dedication and preparation of the pastoral counselor. How will the pastor respond to persons who come to him for help with deeply personal problems? We seek no easy simple answer, for in this way we would only deceive ourselves. No convenient method or typical device will fit the unique complexity of the individual person. To be responsive will require the whole life of the counselor mediating for the whole life of the person.

The pastor will be responsible to the person who comes to him for counsel. His response-ability cannot be ready-made or complete before the person comes, even with all the preparation he may undergo. He must prepare to grow during the counseling hour in response to the specific person in this particular relationship. The pastor himself must continue growing in order to be fully alive and responsive to the person before him in this crucial moment of their history.

In the moment of our meeting on this page, we may indeed

wonder how you and I will respond to each other. What I fear most is a feeble soliloquy of one-way communication where unknown author addresses unknown reader out there. What I hope is that you will respond to me as someone you know, for I am responding to you as to someone I know. Whatever I say comes out of exciting dialogue with real persons who have engaged me in lively conversation. They represent you, and I respond to you as to them in the ongoing conversation of these pages.

My desire is to be a responsive person meeting you as a responsive person. This is what we mean by responsive counseling, where each is continually listening and responding to the other. If this is not quite clear, if what I say is thin or obscure let us continue the conversation from page to page. If you are listening that is good, yet not enough; for you are invited to respond, to break in at any point and talk back or write back, to bring us alive in a dialogue of mutual response each to the other.

To all who have entered the dialogue through the years I must say this word of profound gratitude. And to those who will carry the search forward, the future is yours to decide and fulfill.

Paul E. Johnson

Contents

1
Marking the Boundaries

1. Approaches to Counseling

How shall we approach the subject of counseling? This will depend on who we are and what we seek. This in turn will depend on what we intend to make of it. The question is baffling because it is so complex. In fact, it is unanswerable until we analyze its complexity, sift out the alternatives, and set forth the terms of reference.

If we begin with a historical approach, we find the counselor near at hand in the earliest human societies. Within the family itself the children turn to the parents for counsel; the parents have lived longer and had more experience, so the elders have been consulted by the youngers. The records of ancient civilizations show the procedures of their governments and how the rulers were surrounded by counselors who may have been priests and oracles, sages and teachers, or officers of the court who formed an inner council.

In the historic sense, to seek counsel is asking and receiving advice. Amid the dilemmas of human life this is to acknowledge that one person alone is not sufficient to make important decisions, until he has talked the matter over with someone who will see the situation with him in larger perspective. To avoid hasty, impulsive, reckless behavior we deliberate, or take the time to talk it out with other observers who will exchange views and reason with us. This is so well documented in the annals and historic records of ancient kingdoms and modern states, there can be no doubt that consultation is a universal practice in shaping the course of human destiny.

The *Bhagavad-Gita* of ancient India shows Arjuna counseling with his charioteer who had the divine wisdom of Krishna before engaging in battle. The *Analects of Confucius* show him conversing with rulers and disciples on the conduct of human life with ethical wisdom. The pharaohs of ancient Egypt are shown consulting priests and counselors on how to prepare for life in this world and the next. The ancient Hebrew kings are portrayed in the old Testament as frequently calling their counselors and prophets before embarking upon important decisions.

Yet there is more to counseling than giving advice. If by advice we refer to an intellectual answer or a verbal solution, this will not meet the deeper need that brings us to a counselor. What we need more than advice is someone to stand by us in time of stress. This basic human need is portrayed in every great historic document that speaks truly of man. The deepest despair of human tragedy is to stand alone in the midst of chaos and loss or injustice and enmity, with none to care or stand with him against the onslaughts of cruel oppressors and impersonal fate.

The depth of tragic sorrow is revealed in the Buddha alone under the Bo-tree seeking enlightenment; Oedipus stabbing out his eyes to wander through the world a blind exile; Moses dying on a lonely mountain in sight of the promised land; Socrates facing his accusers and condemned to die by the angry senate of Athens; Jesus in the darkness of Gethsemane and the mockery of those who nailed him to the cross. In such an hour of lonely distress, the human heart cries, "Why hast thou forsaken me?" and seeks desperately for someone to care enough to stand with him.

This basic need is clearly revealed in the biblical view of man. No sooner was the first man standing upon the earth than the Creator recognized: "It is not good that the man should be alone" (Gen. 2:18). When Moses was called to stand before Pharaoh and lead his people from captivity he confessed he could not do this alone. Then he was given the promise: "Certainly, I will be with thee; . . . I will be with thy mouth, and teach thee what thou shalt say" (Exod. 3:12; 4:12). From this emerged the Hebrew faith of the Covenant that a person need never be forsaken, for if he is faithful to God, then he may know that God will not forsake him. This was challenged by the writer of Job, in the distress of a righteous man who suffered tragic losses; yet he continued to believe he was not alone, that God was with him, and "though he slay me, yet will I trust in him" (Job 13:15).

Out of this urgent sense of the right of the lonely person to have an advocate has come the law that anyone who is accused is entitled to have someone stand with him before the court as his counselor. It is in this sense that the New Testament word

Paraclete is translated to read "Counselor" (John 14:16, 26; 15:26; 16:7 RSV). In first-century Greek this was a legal term used of an advocate, defender, or intercessor. Its basic meaning designates one who is called out to stand beside, counsel, and intercede for a person on trial. The references in John are to the Holy Spirit, whom Jesus promises will come to stand by the disciples in his stead. The implication is that during his earthly ministry Jesus had been God's Counselor with men, pleading God's cause with them and representing them before God. In telling them of his departure he says, "I will pray the Father, and he will give you another Counselor, to be with you for ever, even the Spirit of truth" (John 14:16).

Such a counselor is far more than one who gives advice. He is one who cares enough to be with you in the hour of distress and trial, who knows what you feel and understands your predicament, who is faithful to stand up for you and remain with you when others turn aside and desert you. Jesus had said, "I am not alone, for the Father is with me" (John 16:32). He goes on to say you need not be alone either, for there will always be a counselor, a spirit of true understanding to be with you.

When we come to define counseling, these two historic traditions will inform and enrich our view of the counselor. The first definition of counselor in most dictionaries is "one who advises; an adviser." To seek counsel in this sense is to acknowledge the need for wisdom by consulting and deliberating with another person. This continues to be a leading expectation, that counseling will enlarge understanding and enable one who has clearer insight to make wiser decisions.

The other historic stream is the profound emotional need for someone to stand with the lonely person in time of stress.

This is the religious meaning of the Hebrew Covenant in the Old Testament and the theology of the Holy Spirit in the New Testament. It has come to be the essence of justice in the legal sense that every person is to be heard and have the right of counsel, that someone shall stand with him as he comes to trial. These two characteristics of wisdom and faithfulness are required of counselors in our time, with the special training and authority to give professional help to other persons.

In this historic perspective, counseling may be defined as a relationship in which one person seeks to help another grow in self-understanding and ability to follow a responsible course of life, which best fulfills his sense of value and purpose in community with the fellow beings of his world.

If we take this as our working hypothesis of counseling, we have no simple task to fulfill these expectations. Searching analysis will be needed, drawing out what is implicit to become explicit in forthright propositions, to be submitted to experimental testing in practice, with interpretations extending into many chapters and volumes of ongoing discussion. Only a very small beginning can be made here, but if our searching can be joined with the searching of others, we may converge upon a clearer view of the counseling enterprise in theory and practice.

2. *Who Is the Person?*

To be very specific, there are as many approaches to counseling as there are persons who meet in such encounter. Each person is unique in his experiences and concerns. Yet to understand the unique character of the individual person, we must know the context out of which he comes. Where does he belong and to whom is he related? It is through our relationships that we know ourselves and other persons. For no one is complete in himself, and the distinctive meaning of his life is intertwined with the whole web of his relatedness to and expectations of the persons who are significant to him.

From another standpoint it is just as true to say that the quality of the counseling relationship is determined by the persons who enter into it. I am thinking of the person who came for counseling this afternoon, how warm and friendly his greeting, how open he was to talk of his inner struggles, how earnestly he was searching for a sound way out of his blockade, a road to follow in which he can be true to himself and other persons. His spirit entered into the counseling relationship with a sense of freedom to explore the complexities of his life, to state his feelings honestly and work with the counselor toward responsible decisions.

I think of other persons who come into the counseling room. How different they are—each one presenting himself in his own distinct style of life, confessing his dilemmas and disappointments, examining his behavior in relation to the persons who concern him, and wrestling with his destiny as best he can in his own way. Some are more hopeful and others more despairing; one attacks himself and another tends to blame others; one feels inadequate and dependent while another resists authority and strives to be independent; one is sensitive to feelings while another puts his trust in reason; one accommodates to the conditions of life around him while another strikes out aggressively to change the conditions of his life.

What do these persons have in common as they come for counseling? They all experience the acute dilemmas of human life. They are baffled by the tremendous complexity of the situation confronting them: a sense of discomfort under the pressures playing upon them, an urgency about reaching a decision where the issues are not clear, a sharp gap between the ideal goals sought and the meager results in falling short of them, acute or chronic grief over the losses that rob them of loved ones who are dear to them, the anguish of not being understood or approved by persons who are significant to them, a tense impasse blocking communication with an associate or member of the family, difficulty in resolving an inner conflict that defeats wholeness and saps the forward thrust of life, or a determination to work through painful uncertainty to firmer ground and a clearer road into the future.

The person who moves forward in counseling begins to grow in new ways. He breaks through the wall of silence that held him in anxious reticence, to speak forth from the depths of his inner life. He takes a leap of faith to trust the counselor as one who may be able to accept him and understand how he feels. He gathers courage to be a more open person who is able to confess the sorrow he has been hiding within himself. He gains a new freedom to let his feelings come out in the open where he can look at them more objectively with the counselor. He undertakes to look more intently at himself to see what is going on within him. Instead of running frantically away from himself or looking the other way to avoid seeing himself, he now takes himself on and begins to confront himself.

Cautiously at first, and little by little, he can put aside the defensive mask by which he has been shielding himself from other persons. Learning to trust the counselor as a safe person who does not strike back or reject him for what he says or cut him down to size with belittling comments, he is able to be himself. He can relax some of the tensions that distort his perceptions, and letting go the squint in his eye, he can see himself more honestly. As he comes to accept himself he can let himself be what he is, and live his life more truly with a transparent integrity.

These changes will begin to affect his relation to other persons with whom he associates at home, at work, and in the community. Instead of sparring with them to protect himself and gain some private advantage, he can relax his defenses and meet them in freer, more natural and genuine encounter. He is now able to let other persons be what they are because he is willing to be what he is. Instead of manipulating them toward his goal or moving them into a favorable position along the direction of his agenda, he respects their right to set their own goals even though these are quite different from his own.

With these accepting attitudes toward other persons, it is more possible to remove the blocks and barriers and enter more freely into open communication. In this way we reduce the pressures and tensions among us; we see each other more clearly and cherish the essential differences that permit each person to be unique in his own right.

This is not the individualism of my self-interest conflicting with your self-interest in bitter, unyielding resistance. It is rather the unity of persons who respect each other enough to affirm the distinctive life of the other to be as significant as one's own. This is not the anarchy of letting each other alone with nothing to share, where each struggles only for his own advantage. It is rather the truer democracy that values the other person as much as one's self, where each person cares for the other and helps to provide the opportunity for him to fulfill his aspirations and destiny in a community of mutual concern.

The dynamics of interpersonal relations are reciprocal and centrifugal. From the first moment of meeting, counseling is a two-way relationship. Whoever the person may be and whatever the problem he brings to the counseling room, he will give forth a dynamic energy to the counselor. And likewise the counselor, whoever he may be and whatever the viewpoint from which he works, will be giving a stream of his own vital energy to the person before him. Wherever there is transference of energy from one person to another, there will be counter-transference of psychic energy returning to the first person. Otherwise the time is wasted and the effort to hold a meeting is empty and futile. The accepting and understanding attitude of the counselor enables the person to understand and accept himself in a new sense.

And there is going to be transfer of learning from the counseling relation to other relationships. When a person learns through counseling to know and accept himself more truly, he will take these discoveries home with him to his family. As he becomes a new person in the growing insights and awareness of counseling, he will learn to be a new person in the many other relationships of his outgoing life. The effect of counseling does not end with the hour, but goes forth from this hour to all the hours of the person's quest to find himself and be himself in every situation. Nor does the counseling end when the series concludes, for as in all education, the end of the course is in reality the commencement of a new life in the world. Even as the person has been transferring what he has learned from others to the counselor, so as day follows day into avenues of endless growth, the person will transfer what he learns from the counselor to the other persons with whom he lives and has his being.

In this longitudinal view of growth through relationship we can see that the person going forth from counseling is not the same as the person who entered into it. If a growing person is changing through the momentum of every experience and transaction of his daily life, we will not be surprised to find him a changed person after counseling. The nature and significance of his changes will be an intricate product of the counseling plus all the events and relationships of his ongoing life. Which events are most decisive will need to be investigated in the unfolding story of each unique person within his total relationships. The counseling will be only one of these many intersecting events, yet it may actually have a multiplying effect, if it has a decisive influence upon the other events of this person in his social relations. If the person brings to the counselor the really significant events of life for searching appraisal, and if the person carries from this counseling a new life into his relation with other persons and events, we may find the change is very considerable. Whatever change is most far-reaching will not be the outcome of an isolated experience or a single decision. It will rather be the ongoing course of many decisions in reference to the unbroken succession of growing experiences which engage the whole person in modifying and intensifying the overall meaning of his life.

The person who grows through counseling must be willing to grow. He will be a person who desires change more than the *status quo* he has been defending. The courage to grow is one of the great heroic achievements of man, who will otherwise be a helpless victim of the strongest pressures which overwhelm him. The force of gravitation may appear to be the strongest of all forces, the magnetic attraction of mass. But there are other great forces, such as the volcanic eruption of molten lava under pressure which has pushed up mountains and built islands emerging from the sea. So a person who wants to grow may develop an inner force whose intensity prevails over the confining pressures upon him. From this spirit of inner strength he may become the arbiter of his destiny. We stand in awe and reverence before a person who is courageous enough to grow. It is this self-emerging force upon which we rely in every effort, such as counseling, to open the door and clear the way for human growth.

How may we expect persons to change through counseling and psychotherapy? At the Counseling Center of the University of Chicago a careful study was made of the outcome of client-centered therapy. A series of objective and projective tests was given to a group of clients before and after therapy, with follow-up studies six months to one year later. There were twenty-five clients in the therapy group, more men than women, more students than nonstudents, ranging in age from twenty-one to forty. They presented a wide range of problems, from concern over near-psychotic behavior to lack of positive goals, homosexuality, unhappy marital life, failure on the job or at school, difficulty in making decisions, and feelings of social inadequacy. They were significantly more disturbed and less well-adjusted than the control group who matched them as equivalent in other ways. A part of the therapy group was asked to wait during a sixty-day control period. Sixteen counselors conducted recorded interviews with the therapy group. The successive testing of all groups was appraised independently by research psychologists to measure changes in the therapy group as compared with changes in the control group.

In reporting the findings of this four-year study, Carl Rogers notes that therapy brings a change in the perception of one's self and other persons:

> The individual sees himself as entering therapy in distress, decidedly maladjusted, very unlike the person he wants to be. During therapy he moves significantly in the direction of adjustment and integration, becoming inwardly more comfortable and less tense, sees others as more like himself, and relates more comfortably to them. He understands himself better and is more confident and self-directing. He alters his personal goal in a realistic and more achievable direction. There is some data suggesting that the new self-concept includes more of his inner experience . . . and is thus less easily threatened.[1]

When the persons were appraised from an external point of view, the control group showed no change during the period studied. But in the therapy group, twenty of the twenty-five showed personality change in a positive direction from "disturbed" to more "integrated, happy and socially effective."

Changes in everyday behavior were further rated by the client himself and two of his friends from a list of specific behaviors, those which were characteristic of the client. No significant change was found in the maturity of behavior of control individuals or of clients during a no-therapy period. But those who completed a course of therapy showed significant changes which are specified by Rogers as follows:

> We may conclude that the quality of the therapeutic experience is responsible for the fact that, where therapy "takes," the client

[1] Carl R. Rogers and Rosalind F. Dymond, *Psychotherapy and Personality Change* (Chicago: University of Chicago Press, 1954), pp. 418-19.

becomes more mature in his behavior—becoming less dependent, less boastful, less compulsive, less easily upset, better organized, more tolerant, more open to the evidence, behaving in ways that show more concern for the discovery of the facts in the case, more concern for the welfare of all. On the other hand, where therapy is judged by the counselor to be a failure, there is marked deterioration in these same qualities of behavior.[2]

A search is also made in this study for the factors which favor or limit change. Age and degree of emotional disturbance are not found to be decisive factors. Where there are more than twenty interviews the gains are more assured. Having to wait to begin is a deterrent to successful therapy. Clients with moderately democratic and acceptant attitudes benefit most from the therapy. A relationship of liking and respect for the counselor is important. The counselor's attitude should be one of caring, which is not possessive or demanding.

In summary, then, the process of client-centered therapy, as caught in the factual evidence of these various studies, appears to be based on a warm relationship of mutual liking and respect. The client begins with a somewhat intellectual discussion of his "problems" but moves toward a personal exploration of himself and an experiencing of his actual organismic reactions to situations. As he permits more of these actual experiences to enter his awareness, his picture of himself keeps changing and enlarging to include these newly discovered facets of self. When the process is of the sort we have just described, the degree of reorganization of personality and behavior is likely to be considerable.[3]

Such changes as occur through counseling are significant indeed. When a person really wants to grow he may well bring

[2] *Ibid.*, p. 423.
[3] *Ibid.*, p. 426.

himself under the discipline of this intensive and continuous experience of personal learning. And if he does, he may come forth a new person; at least he will understand himself and other persons better. He is likely to be less tense and more open to accept himself and other persons. He will see his life goals more clearly and find himself more confidently able to move toward them. Insofar as he is able to grow inwardly, his friends will find him more mature in his everyday behavior, more tolerant and steady, better organized and more open-minded.

Yet he will be the same person as before, with no break in the continuity of his essential nature. There is an invisible yet very real core of identity in each person which endures through all these changes. This enduring core has been known by many terms; such as spirit, soul, self, ego, or proprium. The soul of a man is no separate part of him over against other parts. It is rather a spirit pervading the whole organism as his style of life. When I refer to myself, it is the whole of me that is indicated and included. There will be changes visible to others through the years of this growing-maturing-aging life. Yet there is an enduring core of identity through all these changes by which we recognize ourselves and our friends.

I once sought to distinguish the *person* from *personality*.[4] Defining personality as the whole human being (me) as seen by others from an external point of view, the person may be thought of as the inner subject (I) who experiences my life. It is the subject (I) who has identity and continuity through all the changing scenes of life. In Freudian terms the I is the ego who serves as executive amid the conflicting forces and counter-

[4] Paul E. Johnson, *Personality and Religion* (Nashville: Abingdon Press 1956).

claims of the id and the superego.[5] In Allport's dynamic view of personality, the I is the proprium striving for goals of one's own choosing.[6] The proprium holds several functions in fusion; bodily sense, self-identity, ego-enhancement, ego-extension, rational activity, self-image and goal-striving. Yet it is not separable from the person as a whole.

It would be fascinating and rewarding to explore further the question, "Who is the person?" In the holistic view of personality theory, the person is the unique individual we observe through all the dimensions and relationships of his growing life. I am not willing to mean any less than this when we study the behavior of a person. And yet when I search for my identity as the essential nature of my being, the person I know from inner awareness is the subject of my private experience. This private experience is hidden deep within me and inaccessible to others until I reveal it to them. They may infer from my behavior what I am feeling and thinking, but the authentic report is only given by the person from his own experience.

This is the profound mystery of a person, that he is hidden in the deep well of his own experience. And yet he is continually meeting other persons who enter his experience and play their parts on the stage of his life. He in turn enters the private life of other persons and participates in the drama of their lives.

Between us we are constantly giving and receiving messages that communicate our experiences and weave the intricate web of social encounter we know as our civilization. In these encounters we learn who we are as persons, interacting and inter-

[5] Sigmund Freud, *The Ego and the Id,* Tr. by James Strachey (London: Hogarth Press [1923], 1961).

[6] Gordon W. Allport, *Becoming* (New Haven: Yale University Press, 1955).

viewing with other persons. We never know all about another person, or even about ourselves. But we come to truer understanding of human life through the exciting and enriching dialogue of person with person.

3. *Who Is the Counselor?*

The counselor may belong to one of a number of professions. He may be a physician, a lawyer, a psychologist, a social worker, a psychiatrist, or a pastor. He will have specialized in one field with a knowledge and competence which sets the orientation of his counseling. Hiltner has shown that counseling is not a separate profession in itself, but rather an activity by which a person seeks to help other persons.[7] In setting out to help persons in some problem area, each profession found that technical knowledge was not enough without a competence in human relations which is counseling.

It is therefore customary and proper to employ a descriptive adjective to indicate the profession in which the counselor stands, and from which he brings his special contribution to human problems. The physician is a health counselor, the lawyer is a legal counselor, the psychologist may be an educational or vocational counselor, the social worker is most often a family counselor, the psychiatrist is a psychotherapeutic counselor, and the pastor is a pastoral counselor.

Each of these brings a distinct contribution from his special field of knowledge, yet all engage in a similar activity of counseling. We have defined this activity of counseling as a

[7] Seward Hiltner, *Pastoral Counseling* (Nashville: Abingdon Press, 1949), p. 95.

relationship in which one person seeks to help another to grow. There are many ways in which a person may grow. One is by eating nourishing food, and for guidance in this we turn to the physician as a health counselor. If we seek to grow through education to prepare for a vocation, we turn for guidance to an educational and vocational counselor. Whatever may be the concern, a counselor seeks to help the person grow in self-understanding and ability to follow a responsible course of life, which best fulfills his sense of value and purpose in community with the fellow beings of his world.

Yet new professions are emerging within the older ones, and counseling may become a full-time vocation. The work of counseling has increasing significance in our time, but always in relation to a field of special knowledge and rooted in a larger professional community. No counselor can afford to saw off the limb on which he is sitting, for he works best as a member of a sustaining community. To this we will return in the following chapter.

The primary focus of this book will be on the pastoral counselor. He will be first of all a pastor who has met the educational and personal qualifications to be ordained and authorized to represent his religious community. Within this community he is trusted to serve the people in characteristic ways; as a priest who leads in worship, as a preacher who declares a way of life, as a teacher who guides and instructs into enlarging truth, as administrator of a parish with its church-related activities, as a pastor who cares for the people in times of crisis and continuing growth. A parish minister may function in all these ways, one of which is counseling. A pastor may have a specialized ministry of teaching, counseling, or chaplaincy in a hospital, prison, or university.

In this relationship of trust, it is natural for many people to come to the pastor for counseling with personal problems. The Joint Commission on Mental Illness and Health conducted a nationwide survey in which the question was asked, "Where do you go for help with a personal problem?" Of all those interviewed in this survey, more report going to the pastor than to members of any other profession.[8] Among those who had asked for help with a personal problem 42 percent went to a clergyman; 29 percent to a doctor; 18 percent to a psychiatrist or psychologist; 13 percent to a social service agency; 6 percent to a lawyer; 3 percent to a marriage counselor; and 11 percent went to others, such as teachers, nurses, policemen, or judges.

These persons were asked: "How did you happen to go there?" Some had been referred by another source, while others had chosen for themselves the person and agency to whom they would go. The path to the doctor or clergyman is a direct one by personal choice, while the other sources of help are usually reached by referral. They had gone directly to the clergyman or doctor because they knew and trusted him, and they thought they had chosen the most appropriate one for help with their particular problem. In going to a pastor they felt they were seeing a person who would give comfort and support, understanding and helpful counsel.

There are only slight differences among the kinds of problems brought to clergymen, physicians, and psychiatrists. Marriage problems are brought more often to clergymen. Most help was reported from the clergy and physicians. When asked how they

[8] Gerald Gurin, Joseph Veroff and Sheila Feld, *Americans View Their Mental Health* (New York: Basic Books, 1960), p. 307. The details of the sample population interviewed and information gathered are reported in this volume.

had received help, 27 percent of these persons said by talking and advice; 14 percent reported help in terms of cure or change in the person and his relationships; 12 percent, help in terms of comfort and ability to endure the problem; 8 percent, help in working with another person in the relationship; and 6 percent, help in breaking a relationship.[9]

This study underlines the crucial importance of ministers and physicians in helping with psychological problems and further recommends that they receive some psychiatric training for that purpose. Since 1925 clinical pastoral training has been given to pastors and theological students, beginning at the Massachusetts State Hospital in Worcester, and now it is offered in more than a hundred hospitals and prisons where the program and chaplain supervisors are accredited. Here the pastor learns with other clinical professions how to understand and minister to persons in crisis, to know himself more deeply, and to relate persons to resources of healing and spiritual growth. The American Association of Theological Schools has emphasized the value of such training;[10] and the American Association of Pastoral Counselors has included clinical and psychological training in defining the standards and requirements for the pastoral counselor.[11]

Without diminishing his preparation in theology and churchmanship, the pastor is enlarging his preparation to understand the emotional needs of persons he will be asked to help. The education of the pastor cannot be superficial or merely academic and intellectual, if he is to respond to the distresses and sorrows, the doubts and despairs, of his people. The people will seek him

[9] *Ibid.*, p. 322.

[10] See the publications of the American Association of Theological Schools, 534 Third National Building, Dayton, Ohio 45402.

[11] *American Association of Pastoral Counselors Manual, 1965-66* (obtainable from the secretary, 201 East 19th Street, New York, New York 10003).

out for help in time of stress and special need, trusting the pastor to understand and give them counsel. He cannot turn his back on these urgent requests. Neither can he turn them away with empty words. He must accept their hurts, listen to their distress, enter into their suffering with empathy and understanding; until, through the depth and sustaining power of the counseling relationship, they can find a clearer way to healing and growth.

4. *Taking a Boundary Seriously*

If the pastor becomes a thoroughly prepared counselor, will he not lose his identity as a pastor? In his clinical training he will learn much of psychiatrists and psychologists who become models for him, and yet who have a different orientation from his own. When he counsels as they do, will he not be acting the role of a junior psychiatrist or practicing psychologist? As he perceives himself to be a counselor and becomes more involved in the work of counseling, may he not turn away from the church and give himself to a secular vocation? There are indeed pastors who have done this and, leaving the church, have entered a vocation in the world.

How will the pastoral counselor keep his identity as a pastor? One way to do this might be to maintain a high wall between his ministry and every other vocation. By holding himself apart from others in his sacred calling, he could accentuate the distance and maintain the separation of his holy office. This might serve as a defensive procedure like the Berlin Wall or the barbed wire entanglements at the western border of Hungary. Here is one way to take a boundary seriously; but it has the unfortunate

ey will need a continuous fraternizing, with mutual ack and forth to see how those in each profession carry vork and how they may collaborate. An interdisciplinary vas held at Boston University for two years with faculty professional schools of medicine, nursing, social work, ogy meeting to learn of each other how to cooperate in e person who is seeking help. And this was only a

toral counselor must give of himself freely enough to the concerns of the other helping professions. He will ithfully with them both in the work of training and f serving; yet he will keep the boundaries clear and h is his side of the border. He will know his field, e the limits of his competence, and refer persons to sions for services they can better give. He will be at pastor in the ministry of his church, neither hiding identity nor evading his pastoral responsibility. He ho he is and the community he is to represent in his vork. There is no blurring of horizons or erasing of vhen the pastor seeks out of his ministering vocation rsons; for they will know, as he knows, that he is a selor.

ctive context of pastoral counseling has been investi- tner and Colston in a two-year research project.[12] hey mean that which differentiates the pastor's om that of other counselors. They identify four the pastoral context: (1) the setting of the church g it symbolizes; (2) the expectation of the person is conception of the pastor's role, function, and

tner and Lowell Colston, *The Context of Pastoral Coun-* Abingdon Press, 1961).

consequences of setting up barriers
rigid control of movement, creatin
all of which cripple and immobiliz

If the pastor wants to know an
he will have to come out from beh
freely with them. If he is to help
will need to be where they ar
suffering. If he is to give help, h
community and the other he
knows them and how they a
adequately serve a person whos
through many relationships.
of the helping professions, a
consulting with and referring
who are in need.

It is better to keep an o
than to build walls. That w
defensive, nor so fearful an
and trust each other they d
over boundary disputes. Th
permit free access across it
seriously, not as a wall to
persons may openly appr
Yet each one knows wher
side of the border is his ho

It is in this sense that a
seriously. He will come
professions who come t
to learn of the other in
sided communication. A
to know each other we

ness. Th
visiting b
on their
seminar
from the
and theol
serving th
beginning

The pa
enter into
associate f
the work
know whic
acknowled
other profe
home as a
his pastoral
will know
counseling
boundaries
to counsel p
pastoral cou

The distin
gated by Hi
By context
counseling f
dimensions o
and everythin
based upon

[12] Seward Hi
seling (Nashville

ness. They will need a continuous fraternizing, with mutual visiting back and forth to see how those in each profession carry on their work and how they may collaborate. An interdisciplinary seminar was held at Boston University for two years with faculty from the professional schools of medicine, nursing, social work, and theology meeting to learn of each other how to cooperate in serving the person who is seeking help. And this was only a beginning.

The pastoral counselor must give of himself freely enough to enter into the concerns of the other helping professions. He will associate faithfully with them both in the work of training and the work of serving; yet he will keep the boundaries clear and know which is his side of the border. He will know his field, acknowledge the limits of his competence, and refer persons to other professions for services they can better give. He will be at home as a pastor in the ministry of his church, neither hiding his pastoral identity nor evading his pastoral responsibility. He will know who he is and the community he is to represent in his counseling work. There is no blurring of horizons or erasing of boundaries when the pastor seeks out of his ministering vocation to counsel persons; for they will know, as he knows, that he is a pastoral counselor.

The distinctive context of pastoral counseling has been investigated by Hiltner and Colston in a two-year research project.[12] By context they mean that which differentiates the pastor's counseling from that of other counselors. They identify four dimensions of the pastoral context: (1) the setting of the church and everything it symbolizes; (2) the expectation of the person based upon his conception of the pastor's role, function, and

[12] Seward Hiltner and Lowell Colston, *The Context of Pastoral Counseling* (Nashville: Abingdon Press, 1961).

consequences of setting up barriers which block travel, imposing rigid control of movement, creating fear, suspicion, and hostility; all of which cripple and immobilize the freedom of life.

If the pastor wants to know and serve the people around him, he will have to come out from behind defensive walls and mingle freely with them. If he is to help persons with their problems, he will need to be where they are and enter into their joy and suffering. If he is to give help, he must know the resources of the community and the other helping professions. For until he knows them and how they are prepared to help, he cannot adequately serve a person whose needs are complex and extended through many relationships. Pastoral counseling will be one of the helping professions, and the pastor can help better by consulting with and referring to the other professions for persons who are in need.

It is better to keep an open boundary with mutual respect than to build walls. That way people are not so possessive and defensive, nor so fearful and suspicious. Where people respect and trust each other they do not waste their energies in fighting over boundary disputes. They mark the boundary well and then permit free access across it to and fro. They take the boundary seriously, not as a wall to divide, but as a meeting place where persons may openly approach each other from all directions. Yet each one knows where he dwells; he does not forget which side of the border is his home.

It is in this sense that a pastoral counselor will take a boundary seriously. He will come from his side to meet those from other professions who come to him from their side. Each will desire to learn of the other in the open dialogue of two-way or many-sided communication. And much time together will be needed to know each other well enough to communicate in true open-

convictions; (3) the shift in relationship from pastor and congregation to the one-to-one relationship of counseling, which is reversed after the counseling is concluded to a parish relationship again; and (4) the distinctive aims and limitations of the pastor in counseling. As pastor he aims at "total redemption" of the "total person." Yet if he is wise he will not push a person where inwardly he is unable to go. In counseling he will face self-imposed limitations as well as realistic limitations of time, skill, and training.

To explore the effects of this context upon counseling, Hiltner and Colston constructed the following design. Lowell Colston, an ordained minister, was a counselor at the Bryn Mawr Community Church and also at the Counseling Center of the University of Chicago. The design was for Colston to counsel matched pairs of ten counselees at the church and ten clients at the counseling center. Actually fifty-nine persons were seen by Colston for a total of 573 interviews during the two-year period; and, of these, twenty-five persons with a median age of thirty-four were included in the study. Thirteen persons were counseled at the church for a median of twenty-one interviews each; and twelve persons were counseled at the counseling center for a median of fourteen interviews each. They were given psychological tests before and after the counseling, with a follow-up interview six months after the close of counseling. The interviews were tape-recorded and analyzed. Ratings of change and outcome were made by the counselor and the counselees. Six cases were selected for intensive study; the other nineteen were sketched and analyzed for clues.

The hypothesis was that persons seeking counseling help from a pastor tend to progress slightly farther and faster in the same amount of time than they would in another setting, such as a university counseling center. This hypothesis is supported by the evidence. The testing shows a barely significant advance by the church counselees over those of the university counseling center. The church people rated themselves an average 3.08 on change and 7.08 on outcome, while the center people rated themselves 2.50 on change and 6.80 on outcome of the counseling. The counselor rated the church people an average 1.66 on change and 6.08 on outcome, while he rated the center people 1.50 on change and 5.90 on outcome.

With the same counselor at work in two centers and employing so far as possible the same method, these variations seem to be attributable to the difference in the context. The researchers recognize that the context will mean different things to different people. Yet if persons seek help of a pastor at all, the change and outcome of counseling will be no less, and it may be more, favorable than in another context. Not every pastor will be equally well prepared to counsel, but insofar as he is prepared, the church will be no deterrent and may actually facilitate effective counseling.

In this situation the counselor was at work on both sides of a boundary. In the church he was perceived as a counseling pastor, and in the counseling center he was perceived as a counseling psychologist. This could be confusing and deceptive if the roles were antagonistic or contradictory. But in this case the roles were harmonious, and the counselor could be true to himself and perform each task and role with integrity.

It is essential, moreover, for the counselor to have such a clear sense of identity that he will not mistake who he is. Colston was always clear in his own mind that his primary identity was that of a minister, in whatever context he might be. He did not flaunt this role of the minister outwardly, yet inwardly he knew this was his ultimate allegiance; and when asked, he did not hesitate to say that he was a minister. This identity he felt as deeply when teaching and counseling as when preaching or leading worship. Under typical circumstances the role of the minister is best fulfilled when his identity is equally as clear to others as it is to himself.[13]

[13] Edward E. Thornton in his book *Theology and Pastoral Counseling* (Englewood Cliffs, N.J.: Prentice-Hall, 1964) asks, "Are the boundaries secure?" His conclusion is that the boundaries between theology and the behavioral sciences are open, not to defend one against the other, but to interpenetrate and homogenize.

2
The Ground on Which the Counselor Stands

1. The Basis of Human Relations

In marking the boundaries of counseling we have noted that every counselor belongs to a community where he is known and trusted. The lawyer belongs to a legal community by whom he is educated, examined, and authorized to be a counselor-at-law. The physician belongs to a medical community by whom he is admitted to medical school, prepared through years of arduous academic, laboratory and clinical training, until he is licensed by a board of examiners to practice medicine.

The pastor belongs to a religious community without whom he would be unable to do his work. Through the encouragement and guidance of his religious community he pursues a required education. He is examined for personal and theological qualifications; admitted, first on trial, and then, if finally approved, is given his credentials to carry on the vocation of a minister. He is recognized first by the local church of which he is a member or the one in which he may be called to serve and by which he is supported in his work. To be ordained as a minister-at-large, however, he must fulfill the expectations of and be accepted by the wider authority of his denomination.

The ground upon which he stands is his relatedness to a community where he is known and sustained. Otherwise he has nowhere to stand in the family of man. This is true of every person, but especially of those who work in the field of human relations.

In our Western world the three traditional professions have been theology, law, and medicine. Along with the humanities they were the main branches of learning in the medieval universities; and those who entered these professions were preparing to give competent service to their fellow men as scholars and practitioners. These highly trained workers were educated and authorized by their professional societies; yet they were also responsible to the larger community wherein they dwelt.

This shows how communities intersect and surround each other in our plural society. A person is best known in a small group, such as the family, work, or recreation group. Yet we each belong to more than one group. The primary group is the one in which we are most at home, but we usually hold membership in several groups that are important to us for a variety of reasons. As our relationships expand through many interests and associations, we enter into enlarging responsibilities. These multiple relationships give us more ground to stand on, with increasing complexity of many engagements and involvements that pull us out in diverse and often conflicting responsibilities.

A Methodist minister, for instance, will be responsible for a local church with its many organized groups and activities, in most of which he is expected to participate regularly. He will also be responsible for his family and the many activities and group associations of each member. At the same time he is responsible to the Annual Conference and various committees and activities of the conference program. The program of his local church and conference will be guided by the actions of the General Conference, the boards and agenda of The Methodist Church around the world. He will also participate in ecumenical ministers' associations, and councils of churches on local, state, national, and world levels. And there will be the many civic, political, artistic, social service, and financial responsibilities to his town, state, nation, and world community.

We begin to wonder how a person can cover so much ground and yet stand firm on his own ground. Pastors are often breathless in frantic and exhausting efforts to keep up with so many good activities. The pastoral counselor will add to these other activities the special responsibility of counseling the persons who ask for this help. To do this he will have to make time in a busy schedule for special training, hours of counseling, writing interviews, evaluating the needs and potentialities of his counselees, and considering with other counselors how to proceed and when to refer to other helping resources.

The majority of pastors add this arduous counseling load to their other parish responsibilities. Consequently, they face the limitations of time, intensity, and duration of the counseling. To cope with distraction and overload, a division of labor is increasingly distributed among specialized ministries. A local church may add another minister to the staff with special competence and responsibility for counseling. Pastoral counseling centers are founded by churches and councils of churches, where ministers with special training in counseling work as a staff in collaboration with consultants in psychiatry, psychology, social work, law, etc. Pastoral counselors who have competent training are recognized by other professions as valuable colleagues in meeting the mental health needs of the community.

With such wide diversity, however, in the qualifications of pastoral counselors, how shall we know who is competent? To cope with the confusion in this rapidly evolving ministry to emotional needs, we must define standards and outline the qualifications of the pastoral counselor. Since 1963 the American Association of Pastoral Counselors has undertaken to define standards by which to guide the pastoral counselor. We will return to these standards in another chapter, but there is one issue particularly relevant to our present discussion. That is the issue of private practice.

When a doctor or psychologist offers to help people through private practice, he must be certified by a Board of Examiners who investigate his competence and give him authority to carry on this work. Otherwise, the people who consult him may suffer at the hands of a quack who is not well qualified to practice medicine or psychology. So this is a matter of public concern to be regulated by state law. The question now arises, will it be appropriate for the pastoral counselor to enter into private practice? If so, to whom will he be accountable for the quality of his counseling service?

The American Association of Pastoral Counselors has defined private practice as fulfilling any one of the following conditions:

1. Working in isolation, without professional or interprofessional consultation.

2. Working apart from administrative responsibility to any organization.

3. Working apart from responsibility to a faith group.

At the annual meeting in Chicago, April 24, 1965, the members of the association voted to oppose the private practice of pastoral counseling so defined. "Members who engage in such pastoral counseling are subject to disciplinary action and suspension from membership by the Committee on Professional Concerns." [1]

The basic issue, as seen by this association, is "accountability for one's total ministry, whatever its setting. . . . In the final analysis, accountability for one's ministry is to the denomination or faith group which ordains a man and continues his ministerial credentials." [2]

It is the responsibility of each denomination to define what it regards as the proper accountability of its clergy. The denominations are encouraged by the association to explore and experiment with new forms of pastoral care and counseling, and to consider what they will regard as a legitimate ministry. Letters of endorsement from the denomination or faith group will continue to be required of all applicants for membership in the association.

This action recognizes that a counselor must have ground to stand upon; i.e., he must be related to a sustaining community where he is known and trusted. The authority to serve as a pastoral counselor is to be granted by the faith group or denomination, and this is the primary community to whom he is responsible. He will serve the geographical community in which he lives and will, no doubt, have membership in professional and other societies. But he is rooted and grounded primarily in

[1] *American Association of Pastoral Counselors Manual,* 1965-1966, p. 16.
[2] *Ibid.,* p. 15.

his church, the sustaining community that calls and authorizes him to carry on this work. His practice is not regulated by the state, as in the case of the physician and the psychologist, for there is a legal separation of church and state. But he is equally accountable for his qualifications and his work to a supervising community where he must be known and trusted.

2. *Interpersonal Psychology*

Every counselor who offers to serve in the area of human relations must himself be well related. For it is his work to enter into sustaining relationship with lonely and distraught persons who seek a living community. Counseling is the interpersonal vocation; not turning away from but toward persons; not passing by, but meeting face to face, where time and place have been reserved to work through the stresses and searchings of personal life. The counselor is there to listen to these searchings, to accept the person more fully, to see the complexity of life, and to consider its meaning together.

The counselor responds to fear and doubt with basic trust and honest truth. He does not use a knife, a ruler, or a hammer as other workmen may. He refrains from every effort to push, pull, or manipulate. He simply offers himself as one who cares enough to listen and join in the search for the meaning of life. He gives himself, within the limits of counseling, with full attention and devotion to the concerns of the other person.

He relies most of all upon interpersonal relations, for he finds in them the source of growth into fuller life. They are the substance of counseling, that which binds together and that which releases the person to be himself. These relations are the lenses we focus and through which we gaze upon the good and evil of life. They are the media of communication where barriers need clearing away to open channels for loving care and healing of spirit.

For all this we need interpersonal psychology. No one can be a person in isolation. He becomes a person in knowing other persons. He learns from others in exciting encounter. He grows through his living relationships in the giving and receiving of the interests of life. In various ways we signal to each other that we desire to communicate. Alternately we address and respond to each other until we invoke continuing dialogue and call the other forth into the life of a person.

One can possess and absorb things, clothe the body and build a house for shelter, eat and digest food. But only as you meet another person do you become a person. As Tillich says: "Personal life emerges in the encounter of person with person and in no other way. . . . [Here] he experiences the limit which stops him in his unstructured running from one 'here and now' to the next and throws him back on himself." [3]

Is this a new way of looking at the person? It seems so obvious that we wonder how anyone could deny it. Perhaps, as William James said of pragmatism, the interpersonal view in psychology is a new name for some old ways of thinking. Psychologists have been so busy looking at segments of life, such as a reaction time or a muscle twitch, that they have not had time to look at life as a whole. Taking an exact measurement is a difficult feat in any science and seems to require stopping the ongoing, interacting course of life to isolate the subject. Even when a psychology of personality tries to deal with the individual person as a whole,

[3] Paul Tillich, *Systematic Theology* (Chicago: University of Chicago, 1963), III, 40, 58.

it sets him apart from other persons like a specimen in a frame.

But we have already lost the unique meaning of this person's life when we isolate him from other persons. He is what he is, and he moves toward what he seeks to become, in reference to and in relationship with other persons. Since 1944 I have been developing this view of interpersonal psychology. Persistently I have been declaring that the person will always find himself in relation to other persons. He is not complete apart from the expectancies and responses of interacting life. Held apart by himself, he may appear to be independent and self-sufficient for the moment. But the appearance is deceptive, for he continues from moment to moment the life and behavior he has learned with other persons. His whole style of life is so integrated with other persons, he will imagine they are present. He will set his goals and behave as if they were looking; he will aspire to what they would approve and judge himself in reference to their standards and expectations.

The founding father of modern psychology in America is William James. During the twelve years from 1878 to 1890 when he was writing *The Principles of Psychology*, he was exploring the nature of consciousness as "the science of finite individual minds" from what he called a "strictly positivistic point of view." Of course this view, as he said, is anything but ultimate. Men must keep on thinking, and the data of psychology must sometime be overhauled. "I have therefore treated our passing thoughts as integers. . . [in] co-existence with brain states." [4]

We note the focus here upon the individual mind, which he keeps apart from other minds. Though he often refers to other

[4] William James, *The Principles of Psychology* (New York: Henry Holt and Company, 1890), I, vi-vii.

thinkers and carries on a dialogue with them, he refers only to the individual mind as the isolated specimen in its separate frame. He acknowledges that minds "coexist with each other in the common receptacle of time," [5] but suggests that of their collective relations nothing more can be said. In considering the relation of minds to other things, he holds the mind apart from everything known in a "thoroughgoing dualism." [6]

The chief method of his psychology was therefore introspection or looking within one's own mind. Here he finds his famous stream of consciousness in continuous change, which is "without breach, crack, or division." [7] In this changing flow of consciousness there is a focal center of attention and a fringe of psychic overtones, suffused and dimly perceived. At the fringes of consciousness we are aware of relations and objects out of range. But the breach from one mind to another is the greatest breach in nature.

Contrary to Freud, who was working out his theory at this time, James denied the unconscious. He asked, "Do unconscious mental states exist?" and replied with ten arguments to refute that proposition, which he called a tissue of confusion.[8] However, he did affirm a co-consciousness which is working during sleep and split-off states in hysteria. He took pains to dispel the merging or compounding of states of consciousness, each of which must be distinct according to a logic of identity. The bare phenomenon, the immediately known, is always a state of consciousness.[9]

This view of affirming only what is in conscious experience

[5] *Ibid.*, p. 199.
[6] *Ibid.*, p. 218.
[7] *Ibid.*, p 237.
[8] *Ibid.*, pp. 162-76.
[9] *Ibid.*, p. 182.

has had continuing influence to the present hour. It is held by the classical personalists and the phenomenologists who say we know only what we perceive in our own experience. But this I find a constricting view that denies the larger wholeness of what it means to be a person.

Dynamic interpersonal psychology will give a larger place to the whole context of relationships in which the person is involved. The unconscious life is continuously engaged with the conscious in supportive and conflicting ways. The transactions with time, space, and objects in the world belong to the whole conscious-unconscious life of the person as he interacts with them to pursue his course of life. The community of persons around him provides the matrix of his desiring, in the give-and-take of mutual address and response. Among persons there is an interchange of experience by verbal and nonverbal communication.

From 1890 to the end of his productive life in 1910 William James continued to wrestle with these questions. Eventually he came to renounce the subject-object dualism with which he began his study of psychology. His mature position was "radical empiricism," holding that experience within the conscious mind is continuous with experience beyond the individual mind. In the article "Does Consciousness Exist?" [10] he set forth his thesis of "pure" or "neutral" experience. Here he holds that pure experience is prior to the distinction of subject and object. The world is "dynamically continuous." Events are co-relational.

May not my whole trouble be due to the fact that I am still treating what is really a living and dynamic situation by logical and statical categories? If life be anywhere active, and if its activity be

[10] This is the first chapter in the volume, *Essays in Radical Empiricism* (1912).

an ultimate characteristic, inexplicable by aught lower or simpler, I ought not to be afraid to postulate activity. . . .

To sum up, mental facts can (in spite of my *Principles of Psychology,* I, 158) compound themselves, if you take them concretely and livingly, as possessed of various functions. They can count variously, figure in different constellations, without ceasing to be "themselves." [11]

Sigmund Freud in these same years was developing his dynamic theory of the unconscious life. His early attempt[12] to explain behavior by mechanical action of brain neurones according to the laws of motion was soon abandoned. He then turned to psychic causation and began charting the course of primary wishes emerging from the unconscious. These unconscious wishes of the id pressing forward in dreams, symptoms, and unwitting behavior are guarded, censored, and opposed by the superego. Between these powerful mental processes the executive ego maintains conscious perceptions of the external world and represses these conflicting impulses in the unconscious. The ego represents reason and common sense in contrast to the passions of the id. Like a man on horseback, the ego tries to guide the superior strength of the horse.

Did Freud view this dynamic mental apparatus as a closed mechanical system governed by such physical laws as the con-

[11] From a notebook James kept (1905-1908) to answer criticisms of his doctrine of "pure experience." See R. B. Perry, *The Thought and Character of William James* (Boston: Little, Brown and Company, 1935), II, 760, 765.

[12] "Project for a Scientific Psychology" (1895). See *The Origins of Psychoanalysis: Letters to Wilhelm Fliess, Drafts and Notes: 1887-1902 by Sigmund Freud.* Ed. by Marie Bonaparte, Anna Freud, Ernest Kris; tr. by Eric Mosbacher and James Strachey (New York: Basic Books, 1954), pp. 346-445.

servation of energy? It may appear so in his early writings, but from 1900 on he portrays the individual as an open system interacting with other persons. *The Interpretation of Dreams* (1900)[13] shows how the events and relationships of the day are worked over in the vivid drama of the dream life. All the material of the dream is in some way derived from the experience of daily life, even though condensed, displaced, and clothed in symbolic form. Dreams are the royal road to the unconscious, revealing the transactions with the world of other persons.

These transactions with significant persons are further analyzed in *The Ego and the Id* (1923).[14] The ego is modified by the direct influence of the external world.

> Moreover, the ego seeks to bring the influence of the external world to bear upon the id and its tendencies, and endeavours to substitute the reality principle for the pleasure principle which reigns unrestrictedly in the id (p. 25).

In the building up of character, Freud gives a leading role to identification with other persons. His term for a dynamic relation with another person is *cathexis*. From birth the infant is drawn to the mother's breast in the primitive oral phase. Eventually come weaning and other separations by which the child is denied close relationships with significant persons. The ego becomes aware of these object-cathexes proceeding from the id, and either acquiesces or fends them off by a process of repression. When the desired object has to be given up, the ego sets up the object within the ego. The parent given up is introjected by a

[13] Tr. by James Strachey (Standard Edition, Vols. IV and V [London: The Hogarth Press, 1953]).
[14] Vol. XIX.

process of identification in which the child accepts into himself the identity of the mother or father.

> It may be that this identification is the sole condition under which the id can give up its objects (p. 29).
>
> When the ego assumes the features of the object, it is forcing itself, so to speak, upon the id as a love-object and is trying to make good the id's loss by saying: "Look, you can love me too—I am so like the object" (p. 30).

By this road the ego changes and sublimates the object-libido into narcissistic libido. That is to say, the external relation to the mother is now taken into the ego as the internal relation to the mother. As the child introjects his relation to the mother he enshrines her in himself by identification. If the child is a boy he will come in time to identify with the father as his ego ideal. There may in later years be other identifications and, perhaps, conflicts among them. If his identification with his father takes on a hostile coloring, the relation becomes ambivalent, charged with rivalry and affection at the same time. Out of these relationships and reactions a person develops his own identity and forms his unique character.

> Here we have that higher nature, in this ego ideal or superego, the representative of our relation to our parents. When we were little children we knew these higher natures, we admired them and feared them; and later we took them into ourselves (p. 36).

As a child grows up, the role of the father is carried on by teachers and others in authority; their injunctions and prohibitions remain powerful in the ego ideal and continue, in the form of conscience, to exercise moral censorship. The tension between the demands of conscience and the actual performances of the ego is experienced as a sense of guilt. Social feelings rest on identifications with other people, on the basis of having the same ego ideal (p. 37).

There are points at which we may take issue with Freud, but there can be no doubt he does present a system open to other persons in significant relationships. Successors to Freud have enlarged upon the search for identity (Erik Erikson) and the relationships to interacting persons in a mediating culture (Erich Fromm, Karen Horney, and Harry Stack Sullivan). Sullivan has developed a new conceptual system based on interpersonal relations.

Jacob L. Moreno has since 1914, in Vienna and New York, been at work building a social science (sociometry) and a therapy (sociatry, psychodrama, and group psychotherapy) upon interpersonal relations. His theory of interpersonal relations arose from his awareness of the strategic significance of encounter between persons when they respond to each other with open spontaneity. Social psychologists have also discovered the dynamic meaning of interpersonal relations, where role perceptions respond to the social expectations of others (George Mead, Kurt Lewin, Theodore Newcomb, and Fritz Heider).

James and Freud both focus upon the internal meaning of behavior to the individual person. They differ, first of all, in that James works with the data of consciousness and Freud with the data of the unconscious. Among the schools of psychology today, personalism and phenomenology stand with William James in his stream of consciousness. Personalists like Borden Parker Bowne and Edgar S. Brightman hold conscious experience the only source of knowledge. William Stern and Gordon Allport consider it the major source from which to develop a theory of personality.

The phenomenologists such as Husserl, Snygg, and Combs, are also radical empiricists in the tradition of William James.[15] Not only is knowledge limited to conscious experience, but the behavior of the individual is determined entirely by his own perception within his phenomenal field. Neither external environment nor historical events cause behavior, but the person's perception of his situation in the field of his own conscious experience.

This I find a very appealing and constricting view of human behavior. It has the value of a half-truth in what it affirms, and the danger of a half-truth in what it denies. I, too, affirm the central position of the conscious person, but I cannot believe that all the data and causes of his behavior are restricted to his conscious experience. How can we deny the significant data of the unconscious life or the causal influences of interpersonal relations, even though we may not be aware of them at the moment? How can we overlook the ever-present ongoing dynamic interaction among persons whose motives spring from all levels and dimensions of conscious-unconscious transactions in the whole personality?

The ground upon which I stand will include all these data and dynamic relations within and among outreaching, outgoing, and interacting persons. My position of dynamic interpersonalism does not deny the data of either phenomenological personalism or psychoanalytic Freudianism. What I want to deny are the denials and constrictions of each view over against the other. What I want to affirm is the need of each one to

[15] Donald Snygg and Arthur W. Combs, *Individual Behavior: A New Frame of Reference for Psychology* (New York: Harper & Brothers, 1949). They call their phenomenology "the personal approach to behavior." See also the writings of Edmund Husserl and other phenomenologists.

listen to the other and affirm the major thrust of both. James was dynamic in his stream of consciousness but until his final years, confined himself to a closed system of conscious experience (as a phenomenology). Freud was dynamic in his analysis of the unconscious, but as his successors will say, he did not unfold the greater potentialities of the conscious ego.

Dynamic interpersonalism learns from Freud the incessant work of the unconscious and interpersonal life. From Moreno we learn the capacity for spontaneity and reshaping the conflicting emotions into working harmony through role learning. From James we perceive the dynamic phenomena of our conscious stream, and our need to take the internal frame of reference if we want to understand the person. From Brightman we learn to test the coherence of conscious experience and move in the direction of purposive goals to be chosen and revised in moving drama.

We aim to keep the person central in this ground on which we stand. But never one person alone, for his unique individuality is forever intertwined with and responsive to the uniqueness of other persons. Whatever a person has become is causally related to other persons who enter into his personal life, and whatever he intends to become will be purposely related to the persons who share the adventure of living with him.

Gordon W. Allport has this open view of the person in his personalistic psychology. He concedes that "a genuine weakness in personalistic writing, both philosophical and psychological, is its tendency to sidestep the countless intersections that occur between the personality system and the social system." [16] He

[16] Gordon W. Allport, *Personality and Social Encounter* (Boston: Beacon Press, 1960), p. 23.

goes on to say that if personalists do ignore these interpersonal relations, their basic contributions will be bypassed and disregarded by advancing social science. He agrees with the earlier personalist, William Stern, that the person is open to the world around him.

Allport recognizes that the person is more than a conscious unity. He doubts that any psychologist whose interest is truly centered in the person could work comfortably within consciousness alone. The unconscious processes, reflex processes, and physiological processes are no less important for the unity of the person than the conscious domain of the self. We had better leave closed systems to the realm of physics, though they have actually been outdated there, too.

All living organisms are open systems participating in a larger context of relationships. It is the nature of any system to be "a complex of elements in mutual interaction." [17] And among all biological organisms, it is man who has an openness surpassing any other living system. Is it not strange then that a person should be viewed as a closed system confined either within his own skin or his own consciousness? What Allport insists is that we see personality as an open system, adjusting ever to the changing character of its social context. At the same time we must see that each individual is unique in the "internal and subjective patterning of these contextual acts." [18] Within all these systems of interaction, we come to the point where the systems converge in the unique person.

The ground we actually seek, to undergird the individual person, is a community where persons are known and trusted.

[17] *Ibid.*, p. 42.
[18] *Ibid.*, p. 48.

Here we find each person unique in his own identity, yet seeking to find the meaning and fulfillment of his life in the whole network of his interpersonal relations. For abstract logic a person may be detached, but this is misleading for he never really stands alone. For larger understanding and active participation, we find him in the community of his constellating interpersonal relationships.

3. *Theology of Relationship*

The individual person is surrounded by other persons in his society. Yet he is often fighting against the persons around him. Is it true that the individual seeks fulfillment through these interpersonal relations? He may fight against the whole system of laws and social regulations of family and community. There is evidently a strong urge to resist other persons, and especially those who exercise authority to guide or control us. Every healthy, growing person wants to assert himself against others to express his unique individuality. Persons are not always turning toward others, they are also turning away from others, to be independent and farther apart.

To have a clear view of man we need to see the individual figure standing out from the background of his social relations. Interpersonal relations are binding and restraining. The person fights against them to assert his indivuality lest he be engulfed and smothered by them. The crisis of every young person, as Erikson shows, is the crisis of identity.[19] From childhood he has tried on many roles for size and style. Now as a young adult he

[19] Erik Erikson, *Identity and the Life Cycle* (New York: International Universities Press, 1959).

is faced with a series of urgent choices to decide: Who am I, what do I believe, what does it mean to be a man or woman of my sex, and what shall be my vocation? In each and all the relationships of my life, who do I intend to be?

To fulfill my true identity, I must stand alone if I am to be myself. Other persons are surrounding me with their expectations, telling me what to be, showing what they want me to do, and asking me to conform. Against these pressures I have an insistent, inner need to take a stand, to speak up and talk back. If back talk is not invited or permitted, then I will act out in devious ways my resistance to those who put demands and restraints upon me. For I need distance enough to breathe, and freedom enough from other persons to know who I am. My destiny is personal as well as social. A democratic society asks each person to develop his own individuality that he may know himself, decide for himself, and offer his unique contribution to the whole community of man.

Here, then, we are caught in a constant dilemma. Every person must be a unique individual, yet also related to other persons. It is lonely to be a separate individual, and we hunger for close and intimate relationship to another person. Yet close relationships are binding and even stifling, they are anxious and engaging; they are wearing and exhausting. How can we stand to be so close to other persons in all the tensions of our complex interpersonal relations?

Every person needs solitude to recover from the stresses of human relations. If we do not find opportunity for solitude, we are overburdened with the emotional load of anxiety and strain in adjusting to the intricate nuances of meaning and intention, the interchanging signals in our endless communication. We have an increasing urge to break out of these confining walls for fresh air, to get away from it all, to put distance between us and have a life apart. Periods of sleep are necessary to retire into the depths of unconscious life to recover the deeper resources of inner personal life, to rediscover ourselves for the new day. Times of waking solitude are also needed to meditate upon the meaning of life, to sort out the confusions and complexities of social relationships, to search for answers to doubts and teasing questions, to read and brood over the searchings of others, to invent and follow the creative openings of these many fragments and moments toward larger perspective.

In such a time of solitude we may discover a profound and tragic insight. The ground on which we stand is no sure foundation but shifting sand. Human relations in the family may be close, but they are anxious and unpredictable. Now for a moment we are loving and accepting; but in the next moment we are hurting and rejecting, or pressing and oppressing each other. In the larger community we meet only in part; we compete as often as we cooperate; we seek a warm emotional response and find instead uncaring indifference. Even as we hope for enduring relationships, we know the shadow of death and separation will overtake us at the end.

The greater life to which we aspire cannot be fulfilled in the local community. We continue to seek more ultimate gound for the human spirit. It is the dimension of spirit that distinguishes man from every other animal. No man can be satisfied with a spiritless and aimless existence. It is not for want of trying, that we are empty after exploring and experimenting with the other dimensions of our earthly life. So we turn to the religious quest along one of the many paths marked by the historic faiths.

Even here, the spirit of man may wander and thirst in the wilderness of lostness and discontent.

When we come to a counselor we are usually seeking a better way to fulfill the human spirit. We wrestle with our personal destiny in the toils and difficulties of our earthly life. Along the course of personal counseling, we analyze the human predicament in which we find ourselves, and though we begin with local problems in the family, we press on toward the larger issues of our ultimate concern. Brief counseling may settle local concerns, but the deeper we go in counseling the more ultimate is the ground we seek.

If we come to a pastoral counselor, we may be openly seeking a theological answer to the dilemmas of our human existence. For the pastor is at work on these human boundaries where we ask theological questions and search for the larger meaning of the human venture. The spirit of man has a capacity for transcendence, for rising above the one-by-one data and details of existence into a larger perspective, for seeing the overall meaning and holding the flux of moments and events in a unity of dynamic wholeness. With this spiritual capacity to transcend the local, we seek a more far-reaching universal dimension of human destiny. The pastor is prepared to "inter-view" this transcendent quest with the person in counseling by a theological method known as correlation.[20]

Theology asks the questions implied in human existence, and seeks the answers implied in the self-manifestation of the divine or ultimate Being responding to man. In the physical world we find a responsive universe where everything is so related to everything else that each event calls forth an answering response. So in the spiritual dimension, we who are finite and incomplete

[20] Paul Tillich, *Systematic Theology*, I, 5.

seek an answering response. The first cry of the newborn babe is a protest of lonely distress when expelled from the close-fitting womb into the vast world of empty space and time. He cries out of his lostness and despair for some answering response. He will cry again and again until someone gives him the answer he seeks. This will be someone to care and be there to complete his incompleteness.

There are many ways of seeking for the answering response. The various sciences and arts seek to know what is "out there," to chart or portray the reality that responds to our quest. Every science and art is at once personal and social. The seeker works in solitude, yet he listens to other scientists, and he responds to other persons in all the forms of verbal and symbolic signs which compose the rich interchange of communication. Whatever field or profession we enter, we respond to those who respond to us. And every seeker will at sometime or other ask ultimate questions and wait expectantly for some answering response.

The pastor cannot sidestep these ultimate questions. They are bound to arise in counseling, where the conversations are open and honest enough to reveal ultimate concerns. There will be various ways and different theologies by which we seek to correlate the questions of human life with the answering response that comes from the reality beyond us. The historic quest for God is a seeking for the ultimate Being who responds to the human cry and reveals the true life to us. The great religions of the world have found different paths up the mountain to this peak where God is found to answer the human quest.

In these days the religious teachings of the past are stretched and strained by the expanding universe, unrolled by the advancing sciences. Heaven is more distant in the space age, and hell is much nearer in the atomic age where we teeter on the brink of nuclear destruction. Tillich speaks of the "God above the God of theism," to indicate that what we call God is the God of our local view and finite limitations. Beyond this there is the ultimate ground of our being. This may be called the Abyss in mystical language, to recognize its inexhaustible and ineffable character. In philosophical language it may be known as the Logos, the meaning and structure of the divine life. In religious language the dynamic encounter of inner meeting is called Spirit. In our ultimate concern we seek to stand on ultimate ground, and receive the answering response of Spirit meeting spirit.[21]

But even as a man fights against and resists the persons around him, he will also be estranged from and resist the Spirit we call God. Somehow our human nature impels us to fight against those we seek to love, and to deny what we most desperately desire to become. No theology or view of man will be accurate if this fighting-loving conflict is not comprehended. For in the deepest sense and at the very heart of his being, man is a creature of conflict who seeks to be whole. Both tendencies of his nature seem equally powerful, the forces of destruction waging battle against the forces of accepting love. This contest rages in every person and every relationship, as revealed in the counseling hour.

On the ground of this ultimate conflict psychology and theology meet. We come to a counselor to resolve the conflicts by which we cripple and defeat ourselves. If he is psychologically oriented he will see the conflict on human grounds and search with us for inner and interpersonal reconciliation in a new

[21] *Ibid.*, p. 156.

dynamic response of love. If he is theologically oriented he will see the conflict on the ultimate ground where God meets man; and he will search with us for inner and ultimate reconciliation in a creative response of divine love.

Christian theology for the counselor will be seen as a theology of relationship. The pastoral counselor will confront man in conflict both on human ground and ultimate ground. He will therefore need to be equally prepared in psychology and theology, if he is to help the person find reconciliation of conflict and greater love through all the relationships of life from the local to the ultimate. He will be profoundly moved by the struggle of the person within himself, to find his own identity and to resolve the crucial conflicts within his family, his work, and social life, his resistant and integrative relations with persons of other races, nations, political and cultural differences. Yet he will see each human problem in the perspective of ultimate concerns.

There are many counseling hours when the pastoral counselor does not speak of God. This is not the time for preaching, but for listening and waiting for the person to voice the concerns most urgent to him, whatever they may be. Until the person is ready to bring out his religious concerns the pastor does not force theological language upon him. The pastor himself may feel a sublime embarrassment in saying the name of God until the mood is appropriate. It is taking the name of God in vain, as Tillich shows,[22] to speak easily or lightly the name which invites this awesome presence. This embarrassment may be a silence of tact, or a silence of honesty where faith is the courage that wrestles with doubt, or a silence of awe before the divine

[22] *The Eternal Now* (New York: Charles Scribner's Sons, 1963), p. 93.

mystery. But the time comes to break through the silence and speak in open and reverent searching of God.

To speak of theology at the right moment may be a word of grace, the *kairos* or historic moment when the Logos breaks into our time. This is emphasized by Thurneysen,[23] who sees pastoral counseling as proclamation of forgiveness through Jesus Christ. But verbal speech will not be enough to accomplish the goal of pastoral care. The pastor and congregation must live this theological relationship here and now in the loving, forgiving community. This will mean to accept hostility, conflict, and estrangement as our common human predicament in which we share the guilt and suffer the anguish of it together. Without this context of forgiving love by which to accept the hostile and estranged person into sustaining and renewing relationship, the deepest hurt of the person will not be healed.

4. I and Thou

Human relations are not really complete after all. For every human person is finite and fragmentary, not eternal or ultimate. So his relations are also finite and incomplete. If we are evil we poison all our relationships with evil. If we are fearful we bring the shudder of anxiety into our relations. If we are confused or despairing we infect our relations with chaos and despair.

We seek a higher dimension of spirit that is more sufficient and sustaining than our fragile and faltering existence. We seek to rise above the sordid commonplace of petty conflict, to correct

[23] Eduard Thurneysen, *A Theology of Pastoral Care,* tr. by Jack Worthington and Thomas Weiser (Richmond, Virginia: John Knox Press, 1962), p. 67.

selfish striving with larger cooperation and wholeness. We seek to counteract destructive hate with creative love, to bring a dynamic upreach and transforming power to new life.

Psychology begins with the experience of "I." But I am known only in relation to "Thou." Real life is meeting in address and response, as Martin Buber has said.[24] Scientific analysis, in its rigorous effort to measure the isolated unit, is inclined to take it out of context and reduce it to an abstract formula. Formulas are useful, to be sure, but as Einstein insisted, they are useful only if we see the units in relation to the observer and the whole moving perspective of our universe. The concept of mind is abstract if it is cut off from its relationships which are at once proximate and ultimate. Persons are fulfilled through relationships that come from everywhere and go everywhere.

This is more than theory; it is the life that engages us here and on beyond our ken. If we are fully alive we are sensitive to and aware of persons. To enter living relationships I step forward to meet the other person. In such meeting I make him present, as he holds me in his presence, accepting and upholding me before him. We sense a more ultimate Being in whose presence we stand, whom we address as "Thou." It is not for us to tear the veil of mystery. We who cannot know each other perfectly must recognize our limitations in describing in chiseled words the greater mystery of the ultimate Thou.

To say "Thou" is to confess I encounter that which is not me or mine, but that which is other and beyond. To say "Thou" is also to avow the faith that the other is a Presence who comes to meet me, who listens to my feeble address and responds movingly

[24] Martin Buber, *I and Thou*, tr. by R. G. Smith (New York: Charles Scribner's Sons [1923], 1958).

in the vast depths of invisible, inaudible communication. What we know of a person is finite, human, and incomplete. What we know of the mystery who comes to meet our searching is infinitely greater; not less than what we know as personhood. We may, therefore, refer to Thou as Ultra-Person; not abstract or remote but concretely living and mysteriously present, related to all yet related to me.

Psyche is meeting Theos. In Greek thought *Psyche* was the soul of man, the capacity to know and feel and decide for himself. Before the sixth century B.C., psyche was held in contrast to the nonhuman powers of nature and divinities. Later, psyche was acknowledged to be the religious capacity in man and to share the same kind of nature as the cosmic Zeus. In our time psychology and theology have often been estranged, but there are signs of a more profound meeting. There are, to be sure, theologies and psychologies which ignore and exclude each other.

What we need is a theology of relationship. This is apt to be overlooked by theologians of abstract theories who hold God far-off in a three-storied universe of heaven, earth, and hell. Who is impressed by the *deus ex machina* of the nineteenth century deists? Scientific perspectives may incline us more to Aristotle's prime mover or to Heraclitus' eternal flux within the course of nature and not out there beyond the reach of peering telescopes and endless galaxies of our expanding universe.

God is not "Wholly Other" in a spatial sense, nor yet in a division of nature that Kant found to banish him from all human knowledge as the inaccessible *Ding-an-sich*. If he is there, he is to be found in the nexus of relationships to his creation. Our search for God finds him already here in relation to us. Our theology does not begin with a lonely God removed by infinite distance, but meeting us where we are. The later Barth affirms: "At the very root of my being and from the very first I am in encounter with Thou, under his claim . . . and a claim upon him."[25]

To believe in God is surely an act of faith resting upon limited experience and general assumptions, not altogether foreign in attitude to the scientist's faith in the axioms of his science. He meets the total impact of inflowing stimuli with the ordering of data to make sense, according to the presuppositions of his science. The work of theology arises likewise as a human response to a meeting with that Other who is inescapably and persistently there.

In classical Christian theology it is God who initiates the meeting by his self-revelation to man. It is God who enters our sphere of life and reveals himself to us in direct encounter. Buber as well, sees this revelation as a direct encounter, I meeting Thou. And this is my own immediate experience of the I-Thou relationship in prayer and communion.

Yet for the personalists: Bowne, Brightman, and Knudson; any view of God arises, not from immediate encounter, but a mediated inference from the rational structure of conscious experience. They stand with the early James in largely rejecting the dynamic unity of the unconscious with the conscious, and the intimate perceptive unity of interpersonal relations. Actually, they practice communion in prayer; yet in maintaining the dualistic closure of person from all else, and to bring a rationalistic proof of God, the tendency has been to infer that God is

[25] Karl Barth, *Church Dogmatics*, III/2, *The Doctrine of Creation*, tr. by Harold Knight *et al.* (Edinburgh: T. & T. Clark, [1948]; 1960), p. 247.

over there at the end of a long line of reasoning, instead of immediately here in revelatory encounter.

What seems to mislead us here is the idea that revelation is propositional rather than relational. Knudson held knowledge to be "a reaction on the part of the mind itself," and concluded, "There is no direct and unmediated apprehension of God." [26] If the person is seen as a closed system, self-contained and confined to his own conscious experience, we can only talk about a remote person as It, rather than address him directly as Thou. The intentional thrust of neo-personalism, as I have called my interpersonal approach, is to move out from the isolated person of a closed self-consciousness to an open, interrelating person, who finds direct encounter with Thou.[27]

If we are to meet God at all, we meet as I and Thou. This is not referring to God as an abstract idea in the mind of a theologian like Augustine. Such ideas are forged by men for their own use, like the tilting lances of armored knights who joust with each other in tournaments to test their skill. The true meeting which Augustine found after years of searching was, to him, the encounter of a real Presence. "Thou hast made us for

[26] Albert C. Knudson, *The Validity of Religious Experience* (Nashville: Abingdon Press, 1937), pp. 98-99; and *The Doctrine of God* (Abingdon Press, 1930), pp. 102-3.

[27] James E. Will explores these issues critically in his "Implications for Philosophical Theology in the Confrontation of American Personalism with Depth Psychology," unpublished Ph.D. Dissertation, Columbia University, 1962. His concluding words are: "The movement toward more adequate empirical definition of the person within personalism is already far advanced by the work of Paul Johnson. Personalism as a whole will be able to follow his lead if it deliberately becomes the theology it implicitly is. . . . Dean Walter Muelder has written of using personality as an 'exploratory principle.' This sounds exactly right in contrast to . . . a final metaphysical principle. . . . When the concept of human personality is released from the rigid tension of trying to do duty for God, it can make a proper contribution to the metaphysical task which Christian theology always has before it" (p. 319).

thyself; and our hearts are restless until they find rest in thee." [28]

What he comes to find is that God's revelation is no word, but his total self-giving to man. Revelation is not an idea or doctrine about God, but a personal relation to God. In the biblical view, God is known in a direct relationship, not as an inference but a Presence.[29] The Incarnation is the self-disclosure of God in man to open fuller communication with man, and from man to man in accepting and forgiving love.

Christ is the Mediator who brings to man the reconciling love of God. In him and through him we find the way of forgiving love, a knowledge of this faithful unconditional love, the unmerited yet unfailing love of God. The cross is central in this theology of relation, for as Jesus was hanging on the cross he was forgiving the enemies who crucified him. In this revelation of forgiving love, known in the New Testament as *Agape*, the shadow of the cross joins God to man in the vertical dimension, even as it joins man to man in the horizontal dimension. It is this manifestation of forgiving love that enables the lonely man to love his fellowman as God loves us. "Private Christianity is not Christianity at all," as Barth says.[30]

We may outline the theology of relationship as follows:

1. God creates man.
2. Man rebels against God.
3. Both suffer conflict.
4. God forgives man.
5. Community of love.

[28] Augustine, *The Confessions,* Book I, chap. 1.

[29] John Baillie, *Our Knowledge of God* (New York: Charles Scribner's Sons, 1939), p. 216.

[30] Karl Barth, *Humanity of God,* tr. by T. Wieser and J. N. Thomas (Richmond: John Knox Press [1956], 1960), p. 95.

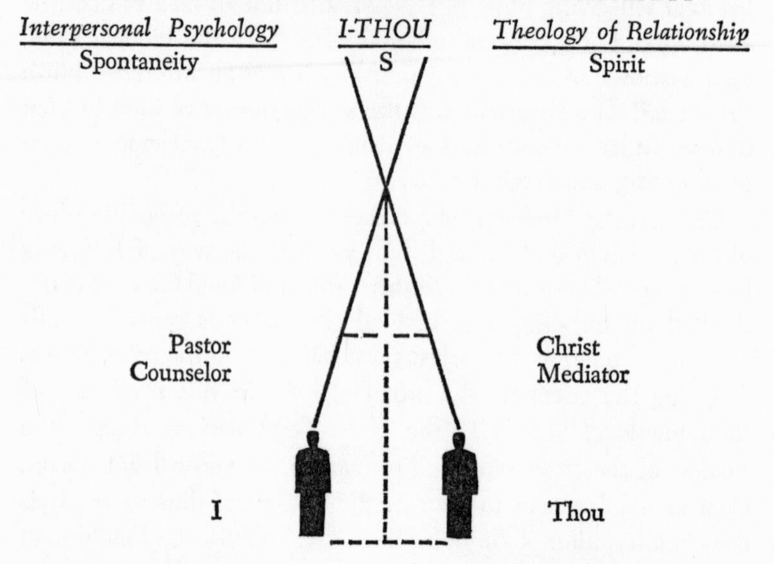

This can be put in graphic form, as we have in Figure 1, to show the psycho-theological ground of community.

Interpersonal psychology meets a theology of relationship. In this diagram we see the I of psychology meeting the Thou of theology. Neither is complete in isolation. I am not a self-contained or self-sufficient monad sealed within myself. I seek among the vast and varied resources of this interdependent world for someone to respond to me. I am not content with the passing throng nor fulfilled in the lonely crowd. I ask for Thou who will hear my cry and answer me, who will meet me face to face.

We cannot know what Thou would be in complete separation as an isolated Being. But he would have no meaning for us, completely unrelated to our lives. He might be the Absolute Idea of the philosophers, but he could not be the God of theology. For theology is always concerned with the relation of God and man. Either without the other is lost in empty meaninglessness or tragic despair. In the dialogue of theological drama, I and Thou are forever seeking each other, and the whole meaning of existence emerges from that meeting.

In our diagram we recognize the dynamic principle of theology as Spirit. Thou as creative Spirit broods upon the deep and awakens man to response. The dynamic principle of psychology may be seen as spontaneity, the erupting and overflowing life energy that moves forth and calls out a response from other persons. The meeting of I and Thou is dynamic, and will have overflowing, ongoing consequences. The S principle will move out from this meeting to other persons and other meetings. When I discover the joy of encountering Thou in a spontaneous spirit I cannot be content with the I-It relation, treating persons as things. I will desire to meet each person as Thou.

Yet the meeting of persons often sets them against each other in conflict and opposition. Persons may resist each other, give hurt, and suffer anxiety. This becomes the burden of interpersonal psychology as well as theology. The way out of conflict is the gracious work of a Mediator, who will take the anguish of suffering upon himself, and bring each to accept the other in forgiving and reconciling love. If this mediating work is to be effective, we must have more than a compromise of differences or a neat formula that is only a verbal solution. What we need and must have is a new and spontaneous spirit to reconcile hostility through a creative and renewing love.

In Christian theology Christ is the Mediator who offers himself upon the cross to bear the suffering of man and God in a passion of forgiving love. This is no isolated incident of a Jewish peasant sacrificed by the cruel tyranny of Roman soldiers. It is central in Christian theology as a crucial event in the history of the world, where the enmity in the heart of man is met by the forgiving spirit of God's love. The universal significance of this event is that the dying yet eternal love of this man goes out, to and for all men, through the forgiving act of God in this and every moment. The spirit here revealed is seen to be the Spirit of God at work in every instant of human conflict and need.

The shadow of the cross falls between God and man, and this shadow stretches between man and man. Our figure shows the Spirit coming forth from the encounter of I and Thou until this Spirit reaches two estranged and all too human persons. Where before they were separated in opposition, rivalry, or indifference, they are now related by the Spirit from above to meet each other in a new relationship as I and Thou. Where before they were resisting each other and suffering painful anxiety, now they come to accept each other and grow in forgiving love.

5. *The Counselor as Mediator*

The role of mediator is both theological and psychological.[31] Jesus came to minister to men and women and children as a

[31] André Godin presents from a Roman Catholic point of view the pastoral Counselor as a mediator. See *The Pastor as Counselor,* tr. by Bernard Phillips (New York: Holt, Rinehart & Winston, 1965), pp. 60 ff.

pastor. He referred to himself as "the shepherd," from which has come our vocation of the pastor. "I am the good shepherd; I know my own and my own know me, as the Father knows me and I know the Father; and I lay down my life for the sheep. "(John 10:14-15 RSV.)" The disciples were called to carry on this pastoring work, which has become the mission of the church to continue the ministry of healing and reconciling love.

The pastor today seeks to carry on this ministry to persons in the spirit of a loving community. Even as Christ offered himself as mediator between God and man and between man and man; so the pastor brings a mediating spirit into the world of conflict seeking a reconciling love. This ministry is known today as pastoral counseling. In our figure the pastor is carrying on the work of mediation as a follower of Christ who comes to heal deep conflict through forgiving love.

To me it is self-evident that all the healing and helping professions in our society are carrying on this work of forgiving love. They accept persons of every age and condition who are in trouble or ill or despairing. They have learned the basic hunger of every finite person for greater love. They know this need for a love to forgive his mistakes and accept him as he is with all his ills and evils. They see him as a victim of deficiencies in our human society, which have left him undernourished in this essential need for tender loving care. They undertake to respond as person to person, and to enlist others to give more love, until the whole community becomes a sustaining and fulfilling overflow of health-giving vitality.

The counselor in every context and profession is the mediator. Wherever he is at work he is mediating conflict within the person and between persons. The pastor shares this ministry of reconciliation with the other helping professions. And he goes farther in his special function as mediator between man and God.[32] This is where the ultimate conflict arises; and until it is resolved, all life and relationships will continue to suffer the despair of estrangement. The pastor must be theologian and psychologist fused in one. He will counsel with the insights of psychology at the same time he is wrestling with the ultimate concern of separation from God.

How can the pastoral counselor be this great? That is the dilemma that torments him day and night. He knows the greatness of the task that calls for such reconciliation. This knowledge brings anguish, for he knows that he is not great enough. He knows the conflicts within himself that cancel his powers and cloud his vision. He knows the conflicting emotions that complicate his relations with every person he meets, and most of all those who are nearest and dearest to him. He knows how his best ministry of reconciliation is burdened with anxiety, disappointment, sensitive hurt, and costly error. He must be able to forgive himself, which is even more difficult than forgiving others.

The pastor is himself in need of a counselor. Yet he is in a position where people look to him for leadership, and where he is expected to set an example in moral perfection for others. This keeps him, reluctantly, at a distance from other people who look to him, and on guard with colleagues in his own and other professions, who might see through him and uncover his nakedness. In this predicament he must find a counselor with whom he

[32] In *Konkokyo,* a modern Shinto sect of Japan, the minister is the mediator who listens to confessions and mediates the spirit of God to men. The act of mediation is central, where the minister serves as counselor and priest. See Delwin B. Schneider, *Konkokyo: A Japanese Religion* (Tokyo: International Institute for the Study of Religions, 1962), pp. 102 ff.

may let down the formal pose to reveal himself as he really sees himself; and work through the conflicting desires and emotions that bind his freedom to help others. For their sakes as well as his own, no counselor can afford to give counsel to others without accepting it for himself.

3
Responsive Counseling

1. Response to Persons

In a universe such as ours we find mutual responses. Wherever we are and whatever we do, we are in the midst of dynamic interaction. If I toss a stone into a pond, consequences follow immediately. Light and sound waves come back to me as I see and hear the splash of the stone in the water. Ripples move out in widening circles from this point until the entire surface of the pond ripples. A physicist has said, "Stub your toe on earth and the impact will be felt on Mars." For the entire universe is one system of interacting events and energies.

This is equally true of our human relations, where persons are continually responding to each other. Every attitude and gesture, every word and tonal inflection reverberates among the persons who live in one household, for each person is sensitive to the signals emitted by other persons around him. If I am sitting on a park bench, says Sartre, and another person looks at me, I am not the same as before. In the very presence of the other person I begin to feel observed and worry about what he might mean by his glance toward me. If he does not look at me, I will then wonder why he is avoiding me. In the course of daily life we move from a family circle to other constellations of persons in which we become aware of their responsive relation to us.

When Mr. March asked to enter counseling I responded affirmatively. He was a member of a university faculty who wanted to form a group to have "open communication on our personal concerns." When we came together there were six of us, four men and two women, including his own wife. There was no agenda but to meet each week for one hour and a half for conversation about ourselves. As counselor, I agreed to serve as convener and to listen deeply to all that was said. I was not to be the answer man, for I did not really have the answers, I said. The leadership was to come from the group, and together we would search for the meaning of our lives.

In the first session Mr. March declared his uncertainty quite openly and cautiously hoped that something might come of these hours together.[1]

M: I have ambivalent feelings about this group, because I have tried so many times to find the answers to what my life really means, without success. . . . Yet obviously there is some hope or I wouldn't be here in this group, even if it is the hope of desperation. . . . And yet I am pessimistic. . . . I really don't expect anything to happen. . . . If it does no one can be happier than I; but deep down inside I

[1] These excerpts from tape-recorded sessions are used with permission of the persons involved. "C" stands for Counselor. Other initials refer to members of the group by anonymous symbols.

have the fear that this too will be a blind alley. . . . I want to find out where I am; and if there is a second step after that, if I find . . . that after all, I am truly involved in this matter of group life here and everywhere . . . it will be wonderful.

G: What you are saying is that you would prefer to be alone, or you would move more rapidly if you were on your own hook.

M: I am on my own hook, and with another meaning.

C: I think he is saying he has lived awhile, and there have been other hopes that have not been fulfilled. . . . It's the way life comes to us. We reach out for more than we hold. . . . So we ought not to hold our hopes too high, because we would not be prepared for the next disappointment. . . .

M: I don't want to be misunderstood. . . . I really want to get down to brass tacks. I am not going to pull too many punches. I am really tired of talking about the weather and how nice the hat looks on you. . . . I want to get down to the basic question of what our life means . . . . and what we are doing, and what it all amounts to.

C: You do seem to be speaking for the rest of us about our hopes and disappointments. And our starting a new group has its mingled feelings of not knowing what will come of it; and wondering if we will actually come through. . . . This is a part of our search together.

H: The way you've expressed it, "What my life means to me" . . . this sounds more philosophical than psychological. And I am not hoping for something philosophical from this group.

M: What I mean to say is that for me there is a great gap between the head and the gut, between the mind and the emotions. . . . I have a feeling that my actions are governed by emotional patterns that lie outside my faith. And that for this reason my faith is not solidly grounded. And this is why I come to the question of what my life means. In other words, am I a teacher because of a clear call and complete dedication, or am I sticking with it because admitting false pretenses would be embarrassing to my family and my friends? . . . I want to be involved, I want to be completely caught up . . . not to lose my freedom in the sense of an automaton, but to stand and speak . . . because it means something, and because I know it to be true, instead of thinking in the back of my mind that these words will be therapeutic to their needs.

C: If this comes out of the depths of our being it is unifying and it expresses what we are.

M: I don't know what I really am.

G: I am trying to find some center that will hold the pieces together. . . . What is the organizing principle of my life? Why do I feel so broken in the sense of going in so many different directions? Not really in control of the situation, or at the center in relation to the children and family. This I feel most acutely . . . and in relation to other people.

Through some twenty-four hours together these persons were searching to know themselves and each other more deeply. There were baffling frustrations and times of breakthrough, when the hidden self stood forth from customary defenses in open revelation and communication. There were resistances, attempts to hold apart, and yet there were moments of rare perception, open honesty, and confrontation.

From this beginning Mr. March asked for individual sessions with the same counselor, where the searching dialogue continued. He is well aware of conflict between himself and other persons. How does he respond to persons with whom he is in conflict? This became a focal issue in the counseling. His contradictory responses were explored in relation to three persons of special significance to him: his father, his brother, and his wife.

Toward his father he responded with fear and denial. His admiration for his father is so great he cannot risk open communication, which he fears might damage the relationship. "My father is a model I want to be like but I can't." There must have been many conflicts between a growing boy and his father. But most of them were so denied and repressed he does not recall them.

Only once have we been in conflict. When I was around twelve, my father discovered a magazine with a bathing beauty on the cover in which I had drawn in the vagina. . . . My father presented me with the magazine and asked if I had done this. I said, "No, Sir," and he went on. To lie was the most serious sin in our family. I did not fear physical punishment but his disapproval if I disappointed him. Even his punishment was in love, and my shame was that I had failed him and betrayed his trust. . . . My home must have been very tense in anxiety over breaking the rules.

Toward his brother, two years older, he responded with anger and rivalry. Here his feelings were acted out openly and aggressively. As he recalls it, their life was a running battle of ever-continuing conflict.

He teased me incessantly. I had a hot temper and would scream and chase him around. He would drive me wild. There were dramatic incidents when anger was violent and out of control. Once I was so angry with him I was pulled off of him when banging his head on the pavement. I would have killed him if we had been left alone.

His relationship with his wife was complicated by the interaction of these contradictory responses. He wanted to be open with her and fully expressive, but she was anxious and guarded. The more he pressed for sex, the more she avoided it. The more he talked about his experiences and feelings, the more cautious she was not to expose herself. He urged that they go to a counselor, and she would say, "You want to change me; you do not accept me as I am." The pressure built up to irritation and anger, which led to acting out in hostile distress the feelings they could not talk out freely. He could say I love you and I hate you; but she could say neither.

Another response emerging from the stress of conflict was guilt and punishment. Husband and wife blamed each other and found devious ways to inflict punishment. Each one could solace his sorrow by projecting the responsibility for the hurt on the other. So there was the guilty party over there, not to be accepted or forgiven.

And yet neither was able to escape the effects of guilt and punishment. Even while holding the other accountable, each was involved in the self-torture of attacking himself. Mr. March could say: "I have been quick tempered with my son, rejecting myself in him. I do not know if I can ever accept myself. This is my deepest concern, and it affects all my relationships."

From the first interview he and the counselor recognized this self-punitive tendency. "I seem to want to punish myself." One evidence of this was his sense of disorder. "My study is a mass of confusion and I cannot clean it up. I become over-extended," speaking everywhere, Boy Scout troop leader, and many other engagements. "When there is so much to do, my reaction is to do nothing. This is painful and I cannot be satisfied until I can bring my life into disciplined order."

Though he claimed no feeling of guilt in some areas of life, he did say: "I feel numb all the time." Again he said: "I don't seem to have any feeling about things where I want to feel." The pain of his guilt was so acute he was unconsciously sealing it off by repression. Yet his anger would not subside, and turning it upon himself, he hated and rejected himself. "I despise myself." Attacking himself was depressing to his initiative and desire to succeed. "Do I want to fail and not succeed? Others find joy in success, but if I do have success I lose interest."

> I seem to live carrying a big placard front and back that says, "If only." And you can't live with this formula. It always throws dust in your eyes. I carry it over into my work . . . into my relationship with W [wife] . . . and I carry it into all my life. If I could take this "If only" off my back, and kill it, and bury it, then I would be going a long way . . . toward security and effectiveness.

He was caught in an interlocking trap of fear, anger, and guilt. Each motive conflicting with the other intensified the anguish of the struggle. These emotions were not playing in a vacuum; they were not hermetically sealed within himself. He was interacting with other persons who held the utmost significance to him. Out of these interpersonal relations came the hopes and disappointments, the anxieties and fears, the hostile distress, and the guilty need to punish himself.

In this network of binding relationships, he was not free to be himself or give himself fully to others. His emotional life was a mounting fever of repressed anguish, a kind of delirium breaking forth in irrational and desperate lashing about. Even the effort to hold his feelings within himself was exhausting and unsuccessful. The pressure within was spilling out to poison his relationships. Especially in wrestling with his wife for love, he had hurt and been hurt so much that every act or omission registered a blow on sensitive wounded spirits.

Was there no way out of the trap that held him a prisoner in spite of his struggle to free himself? There were steps toward separation, as in desperation they turned elsewhere for acceptance and affection not found at home. There was his wife's threat of suicide, her going off alone in a canoe for the day, where the husband was not welcome when he finally found her. There was talk of divorce, which brought them to a respected physician for three months of helpful counseling. Yet the inner separation remained as they lived in the same house and carried on a distant and resentful partnership.

After trying everything and only hurting each other the more they settled into a rigid stalemate of hopeless despair. As he said:

M: There is only one solution . . . not to put any hope in her . . . or any expectations that rest on her . . . to cut off any search for fulfillment in her.
C: So you will not be disappointed. . . .
M: Rejected, despised, and hated. . . . It's one thing to know this is true . . . and another to be reminded day after day after day. . . . Then it is hard to live with.
C: And what do you find is your best stance?
M: To be busy, avoid collisions. . . . Keep my mouth shut.

2. *The Bridge of Encounter*

Real life is meeting. But if persons are to meet in real life, there must be a bridge of encounter. This will need to be a suspension bridge woven together with cables of many basic interpersonal responses. We may think that persons are meeting everywhere they go. But in our society most people are passing by each other on highways and sidewalks without actually meeting at all. We may work in the same building or dwell in the same house in a state of aloof separation.

True encounter is, strangely, the exception rather than the rule in our world of private citizens. Each person has his private life like a castle where he hopes to dwell secure from interruption and intrusion. He may not really know himself very well, or be at home within himself, though privacy is a refuge from the storms and stresses of the world around him. Yet he finds the narrow confines of his private life so constricting he will naturally desire freedom to go forth. How can he bridge the chasm to meet other persons in the larger world?

A turning point came when Mr. and Mrs. March joined the interpersonal group. They both had misgivings, which they were able to put into words. She said in one session, "Let's not talk about me any more; it makes me nervous." And another time he said, "I think you joined the group to keep me from talking too much." Yet they were listening to each other, participating in open dialogue, and often supporting each other in revealing and searching their feelings. As the dialogue continued in the accepting atmosphere of the group, they began to feel differently about each other.

A first bridging cable of *accepting responses* now began to appear. They were somehow, though with difficulty, learning to accept each other. And this was a counterpoint to accepting themselves. In the individual counseling he was steadily working over his feelings toward himself and his wife and his father, until little by little, he could see more clearly what he had been repressing within himself and projecting upon others. Talking it out, seeing and relating the fragments, he began to assimilate and unify his painful experiences into a new perspective. But this could not come about instantly.

M: The problem of conflict . . . can it be overcome by accepting the situation, even without changing it?

C: I think so. . . . And this is the best way . . . the most essential way.

M: It is also the toughest.
C: Yeah!
M: It's the toughest because the elements involved in success are beyond reach. . . . It's one thing to say in your mind, "I fully accept it," and it is another to accept it with the old gut down here. . . . I find myself frequently torn apart.

A second cable in the bridge of encounter is woven of *sustaining responses*. Where there is anxiety and stress we keep the other person at a distance. We may avoid a meeting, turn the other way, exclude or reject him. "I begged her . . . and she said, 'Please let me alone.' . . . Nothing I could do." In many overt ways we push the other person away, cut him off, and let him down. To build a bridge we must find ways to uphold and sustain the other in a supportive relationship. I must be with you and let you be with me.

When we have hurt each other, this is not easy to do. We are uncomfortable together; and the closer we are, the more we suffer the hurt. Closeness may be comforting as a child in the arms of a loving mother, but it may be very painful to receive a hurt and remain close to the one who hurts you. We tend to withdraw and protect from the hurt. "She fears to be hurt if she exposes herself to love." It is therefore a very significant step when a person hurt is willing to accept the other, to welcome his coming and uphold him as present. This was noted by Mr. March in a counseling session.

There have been recent steps toward more acceptance in our marriage. My wife, who has not wanted to change, is changing in significant ways. Since she decided to join the interpersonal group she has been trying harder to find a new life at home. We feel closer and sense we are more together. She has arranged towels and washcloths in the bathroom with a label for each member of the family.

A third cable to bridge the encounter is woven of *communicating responses*. This will come only after accepting and sustaining responses have paved the way. Of course, we may speak to a person before accepting him. But this is a monologue of constricted address. It is not the true dialogue of free and open communication in mutual self-giving. Instead, there is only guarded speech and resistance to avoid confrontation.

When Mr. March lied to his father he was avoiding communication. And he was never able to remove that barrier. In spite of his admiration for his father, even because of the desire to keep a perfect relation with him, the son was not able to break through his deception. In the counseling he came to see how crucial this was in his life and felt he must do something about it. So he made a public confession in a religious service where he was speaking to young people. He told them he was caught in a trap of guilt and separation and promised he would write to his father to clear it up.

But week after week he would report to the counselor, "I haven't written that letter to my father yet." Then he observed, "I always put off writing letters until my friends give up on me." It was sometime later he opened the counseling session with these words:

I finally sat down and wrote the painful letter to my father. I was amazed how vivid my memory of that occasion was. . . . The unforgivable sin in our family was lying; . . . almost anything else could be dealt with. . . . I did not have any physical fear, but I did have a great fear of his disappointment and shame, . . . the feeling

I had failed him . . . and betrayed his trust. . . . That was overwhelming.

I don't know what his reaction will be. . . . I feel sure that he will say that I am making a mountain out of a molehill . . . and he certainly will forgive me for telling the lie. . . . But still there is an irrational fear . . . that he will reject me. I felt this at the time when I was writing the letter. . . . Completely irrational . . . because I don't believe he will; I know he won't. But at the same time I am afraid he will. . . . It will be a great relief to get his answer. I am so glad I wrote the letter because it is working and preying on my mind, that he would die before I could tell him.

A fourth bridging cable is woven of *trusting responses.* Mr. March was finally able to communicate with his father when the weight of his fear and shame was overbalanced by a stronger trust. He had not trusted enough at the time he told the lie, or ever since, that his father would still accept him. Even as he was writing the letter he was beset by the irrational fear that his father might reject him. Yet in his wrestling with this fear he was at last secure enough in trust to take the risk of confessing his lie. His trust was growing through the accepting and sustaining relationships in the group and with a counselor who did not reject him whatever he revealed of his shame and falsehood.

Trust is a very complex emotion, arising from the uncertainty of many contradictory experiences. As Tillich says, doubt is a necessary element in the dynamic of faith. The "uncertainty in faith cannot be removed, it must be accepted."[2] And this takes courage to undergo the risk of faith. The attitude of trust is enriched by the reinforcing experiences of trustworthy relationships, but there will never be complete certainty, and every act of faith will have to emerge from inner wrestling and growing

[2] *Dynamics of Faith* (New York: Harper & Brothers, 1957), p. 16.

courage to believe. Faith will decline and weaken unless there are reinforcing and sustaining relationships of trust. And trusting responses are basic to open encounter.

A fifth bridging cable is woven of *forgiving responses*. There was need for such forgiving responses between Mr. March and his father. The father had often made the son feel guilty by the high moral code he insisted upon. He was the moral authority for his son, who both submitted and resisted. When he submitted he felt it was imposed upon him from above, and not really his own. When he rebelled against the father's demand he was seeking to be his own authority. Both his rebellion and his resentment toward the father would create guilt needing to be forgiven. It would be as difficult to forgive himself as his father in the interacting stress of his relationship. And the guilt infected his relation to God as the ultimate Father.

M: What constantly torments me is that this whole morality and ethical system that is part of me, ought to collapse like a house of cards if the God on whom it is founded is not related to anything. And I don't seem to believe in God. I affirm God intellectually, but he is not real to me. . . . I can't move on from the intellectual to the emotional affirmation of God.
C: Does it seem to you that you ever really confessed to God . . . and had a return to him to find any peace?
M: I have certainly been confessing and asking for this more than one time . . . but I did not feel forgiven. I don't now. . . . I have often thought of that moral sermon that God's forgiveness is already given in the cross. . . . The symbol of God's love is the old father . . . having left the comforts of the home . . . to stand out where he is able to watch for the prodigal son. . . . Today is the day to meet the son. . . .

The Father has already forgiven and it is we who refuse to accept forgiveness, who refuse to forgive ourselves. And I realize this is what the situation is. I believe that God has forgiven me, but I can't seem to forgive myself. It does not mean enough to say you ought to forgive yourself. This doesn't seem to be the handle.

There's no feeling of overwhelming shame. . . . I have always felt I was dead about this, as if it was somebody else's existence and not mine.

C: So this is a clue, perhaps, to work with. Do you agree? . . . Not feeling bad about it . . . and the way it has been repressed more than worked through . . . but something to hide and put behind you. . . .

M: Well, how do you work it through?

C: No mechanical way . . . but it seems to call for intense emotional reliving of the conflict.

When the reply came from his father, a repressive tendency was revealed there too. The father replied that he did not remember the incident. But he did appreciate the son's confession and the desire to speak the truth more openly. He said that if he had known, he would long since have forgiven his son. From that time on there was an outpouring of communication in more frequent exchange of letters between them.

M: I have written him and mother more letters than in a year . . . and they have appreciated it tremendously. . . . Have written to my four brothers and sisters. . . . We were not writing for years . . . and good letters are coming back. In a real sense I have renewed ties with the whole family and high school friends. . . . It is sure nice to hear from them too.

A sixth bridging cable is woven of *understanding responses.* A whole series of insights came to Mr. March about himself as he continued the counseling. What had been denied and repressed by anxiety and guilt, what had been distorted and overlaid by anger and hurt, was now coming into clearer focus. In the midst of one session he said: "I have a deep satisfaction at this moment. Others have so long been saying, You have no problems, go ahead and love each other. Now you see that we have deep hurt to work through; and we can get at it and do something about it."

As he came to understand himself more deeply, he seemed to find a new understanding of his wife. This was not like the burst of dawn, but like stars shining here and there in the darkness as the clouds were swept away. He began to see himself in relation to her as one who was, in part at least, causing her painful behavior toward him. It was at last evident that his nonverbal communication was more important than the verbal, for he was in every attitude rejecting her even while struggling for love.

He began the eleventh session by saying emphatically,

She is not going to change any. . . . I mean, . . . fifteen years I have been hoping and praying and trying to do my best to be understanding, sympathetic, and encouraging; but I don't see any hope. . . .
C: This is a point I think worth analyzing. . . . How to deal with unfulfilled expectations. . . . There are certain approaches you have been making that are not working.
M: That's right.
C: So it seems to call for a new approach.
M: I am willing to try anything. . . . I will do anything if it promises hope, but my mind is completely blank.
C: A new approach that seems to promise more is to revise expectations, according to the clues, the signals, and the learnings that are possible in your life together. . . .
M: That is the same as giving up all hope.

Slowly he came to see that his attitude of hopelessness was communicating a rejection of the marriage. He saw that he was giving her a devastating stream of disapproval in his very silence at the table. As he came to see more clearly what he was doing he could say:

> I know that my silent communication stems from an almost . . . pathological hatred . . . and this is beyond control. I try to repress this, I try to say to myself I can't do it this way, yet I suppose I feel so completely rejected and badly treated by her that I bitterly resent her.

Realizing the pressure of rejection he was bringing upon her gave him the lead for a new approach. A new beam of hope came to him that if he would change his attitude toward his wife, she would be less defensive and more free to change her attitude toward him. He knew that pretending to love and acting what he ought to feel would be a futile hypocrisy.

> Suddenly to push the button and come up with new emotional attitudes is something I do not know how to do. . . .
>
> When we talk of being reasonable, we cannot, because we are caught in deeper emotional currents where we are stabbing each other all the time. Down there in the deeper currents is where the change has to occur.

In order to have a deeper change he would have to perceive his wife in a new light, so he could feel differently and respond differently to her. This would be to understand her as a person in distress, who is desperately trying to hold herself together. If she can receive approval and acceptance from her husband, she can relax her tensions and be more accepting of her husband and children.

All these responsive cables are needed to provide a suspension bridge for true encounter. Words are not strong enough to uphold these important interpersonal relations. If we are to meet person-to-person, we must faithfully give accepting, sustaining, communicating, trusting, forgiving, and understanding responses to each other. Then we can relax in the security of such a bridge across which to approach the other person.

When from the deeper currents of his emotional life Mr. March brought forth these new responses to his wife, she could hear the nonverbal communication. And knowing herself to be accepted and understood, she could be more free to give affirming and sustaining responses to her husband.

Three weeks later when he came to counseling, he said he felt like a new person. "It's hard to express how immense is the difference in my personal feelings to know I am doing my best." He had cleaned up the study, written over forty letters, and worked out a memory system so as not to forget things.

I've developed a new picture of myself as a person. . . .

It has made a difference also in my relationship with my wife. Today along about 3:00 o'clock she said, "I think I will go out and make a Valentine-shaped cake. Does anyone have any objection?" I said, "I don't." She came over and put her arms around me and whispered in my ear, "This is the first time I've felt like I wanted to make a Valentine cake." I felt like saying, "This is the first time I wanted to receive a Valentine cake.". . .

So we seem to be communicating . . . a new kind of dialogue, which I feel is largely due to what you have been able to do . . . either here or in the group. I didn't believe it was possible, but it has made an immense difference to me.

3. *From Capsule to Open Community*

In these conversations with Mr. March we learn how significant to him are the interpersonal relations in his sphere of life.

The dilemmas of his concern arise from his relationships to other persons such as his father and mother, his brother, and his wife. His responses to these persons embroil him in the fear, anger, and guilt of personal conflict. Through counseling he is able to build a bridge of accepting, sustaining, communicating, trusting, forgiving, understanding responses. This working through conflict to personal growth and sound relationships is what we mean by responsive counseling.

Since 1945 I have been seeking to develop a responsive counseling.[3] This approach to counseling emerges from an interpersonal psychology and a theology of relationship. The central thesis is that persons are not complete alone but seek fulfillment in relation to other persons. The counselor offers himself in a person-to-person relationship of accepting and sustaining responses. Across the bridge of this encounter, they seek to understand and communicate what they see and learn in searching together. The goal of this counseling is a continuing growth in all the relationships of the person's life.

Here we stand over against Carl Rogers, whose client-centered therapy has found so much favor among counselors in our time. We are deeply indebted to Rogers for his clear and persuasive exposition of the person-centered theory of counseling, supported by recorded interviews and ongoing research. I personally find much to learn from him in his view that is never static but "constantly revising." He modestly offers "hypotheses to be tested and explored," to provide a challenge to other workers to formulate alternative hypotheses.[4] What he then called non-

[3] This point of view I first presented in "Clinical Psychology for the Pastor," *Journal of Clinical Psychology,* I (1945), 262-71; and "Methods of Pastoral Counseling," *The Journal of Pastoral Care,* I (1947), 27-32.

[4] Carl R. Rogers, *Counseling and Psychotherapy* (Boston: Houghton Mifflin, 1942), p. 17.

directive counseling has been revised to "client-centered therapy" to bring the focus on the person at the center.[5]

In this we rejoice, for the person is well seen to be at the center of his experience and his relationships. But though Rogers explores some relationships with the client, he seems to hold them external and detachable, as if the person may be whole in himself without them. This is the crucial point of difference between us, for I hold an internal view of the relations as integral with and inherent in the wholeness I seek to become as a person.

To Rogers, every individual exists in a private world of his own experience. This private world he calls the phenomenal field; and this self-experience is the only reality he can know. "I do not react to some absolute reality, but to my perception of this reality. It is this perception which for me *is* reality."[6] We are here reminded of the phenomenalism or radical empiricism of William James, declaring that I know only the stream of my own consciousness. We are reminded also, of the classical personalists who upheld a dualistic wall between persons, each one contained within his separate monad. The world within is the only reality I can know directly; all else is inference and speculation.

This self-contained view is graphically portrayed by Rogers in the figure of two circles, one of "Self-Structure" and the other of "Experience."[7] At the beginning the margin of their overlapping is small, but as the counseling proceeds one recalls and integrates more of his experiences, until the two circles

[5] *Client-Centered Therapy* (Boston: Houghton Mifflin, 1959).
[6] *Ibid.*, p. 484.
[7] *Ibid.*, pp. 526-27.

more largely overlap. What is missing here is the other person and the world beyond the self. The aim of this therapy is to enlarge the self, yet in unreal isolation, as if he were not involved with other persons in the surrounding world.

The goal of Rogers' counseling is defined to be self-actualization. "The organism has one basic tendency and striving—to actualize, maintain, and enhance the experiencing organism." [8] If counseling can free the person from his dependence on other persons, he can be more independent and mature. "The organism actualizes itself in the direction of greater . . . independence and self-responsibility." [9] Though he knows there are other persons around, each individual seeks to enhance his own interests independently with as little interference as possible. This reflects the political theory of enlightened self-interest, where the ideal society is a utopia (or anarchy) of noninterferring individuals, each pursuing his own independent interest untrammeled by the concerns of others.

But this utopia is not of this world. It surely cannot be the crowded planet on which we work out our human destiny. There is no desert island or separate star for each person to be at home alone. Robinson Crusoe must have his man Friday to give a human dimension to his life story. If our counseling is truly to actualize the self, it must be in relation to other persons, who enhance the meaning of his life and maintain with him a community of mutual interests.

Rogers speaks eloquently for the right of the individual to be himself, free from the pressure and advice of those who would confine him to their rigid forms. But I find his theory incomplete and misleading. I cannot agree with his capsule theory of per-

[8] *Ibid.*, p. 487.
[9] *Ibid.*, p. 488.

sonality as a self-contained and self-sufficient organism. In cherishing this myth of the individual person in free-floating aloneness, he seems to be fostering the illusion of self-actualizing omnipotence.

So it seems to me that Rogers' theory of counseling is out of this world. It appears that the goal is to launch an astronaut into orbit in a self-enclosed capsule, sending him on his way alone to be himself without interference from other persons. Is this not the daydream of an island paradise where all demands and pressures may be left behind? The fantasy is to float in a little egocentric world of my own, effortless and weightless, as a self-contained capsule in outer space, sufficient of myself to fulfill my own desires.

Does Rogers really believe that persons can be so remote from each other? He does refer to "interaction with environment," but it is the perceptual field of one's own inner experience. He values a "therapeutic relationship," but it is temporary, limited, and detached from social life. He perceives the normal person as self-centered, seeking to satisfy his own needs, to maintain and enhance his own organism. Is this not a sterile and introvert narcissism of I for Me by Myself?

Is this fair to Carl Rogers? No, I think not. He is a very patient man, but he might well be incensed at this interpretation. I would expect him to join in vigorous dialogue to correct my misapprehension. "This is not what I mean. You have misunderstood me."

"You have written clearly," I would respond; "I have carefully read what you say."

"You may have read the words," he would reply, "but out of context, to miss my full intent."

"This," I reply, "is only my perception of what is in your mind.

And your view of what I mean is only a percept within your mind. How can we really know each other, or communicate between your capsule and mine?"

And he will reply as a true counselor, "We must listen to each other more deeply, while we speak of our feelings and perceptions. We must have empathy to feel what the other feels from his internal frame of reference."

And my inclination is to agree that we must continue communicating openly, person-to-person, if we are to accept and understand each other. This is what goes on in his counseling as well as mine. Yet there appears to be a difference in our goals. My aim is to enter into relationships more fully. His aim is to free the person from binding relationships so he may become an independent self-actualizing, self-maintaining, and self-enhancing person.

Rogers has more to say in his recent book, *On Becoming a Person*. In Chapter 8 he gives his view of the goal of therapy: "To be that self which one truly is." [10]

He sees the client moving away from facades and oughts, away from meeting the expectations of others, away from pleasing others, toward self-direction. "The individual moves toward living in an open, friendly, close relationship to his own experience" (p. 173). To be close to his own experience is the goal rather than "open, friendly, and close relationship" with other persons. Yet indirectly this openness to his inner experience may enable him to accept other individuals—that is, to let them be what they are over there, as I can be what I am here.

In Chapter 3 he considers "the characteristics of a helping

[10] *On Becoming a Person* (Boston: Houghton Mifflin, 1961), p. 166. This phrase is from Sören Kierkegaard, *The Sickness unto Death* (Princeton: Princeton University Press, 1941), p. 29.

relationship." In asking how one can create a helping relationship, he gives this reply: "If I can form a helping relation to myself—if I can be sensitively aware of and acceptant toward my own feelings—then the likelihood is great that I can form a helping relationship toward another" (p. 51). To be what I am is the key, and to hope this will show through to the other person, though this "is the most difficult task I know and one I never fully achieve" (p. 51). This he believes will help him to find what has gone wrong with interpersonal relations which have become snarled. "If I am to facilitate the personal growth of others in relation to me, then I must grow, and while this is often painful it is also enriching" (p. 51).

This chapter does reveal the importance to Rogers of the relationship in counseling. He asks searching questions such as these:

1. Can I be, in some way which will be perceived by the other person as trustworthy?
2. Can I be expressive enough as a person that what I am will be communicated unambiguously?
3. Can I let myself experience positive attitudes toward this other person?
4. Can I let myself enter fully into the world of his feelings and personal meanings and see these as he does?
5. Can I act with sufficient sensitivity in the relationship, that my behavior will not be perceived as a threat?
6. Can I meet this individual as a person who is in the process of *becoming*?

These questions accent the kind of responses that we have found essential to a living bridge of encounter. He, too, recognizes the basic need for accepting, trustworthy, sensitive, positive, open, and communicating attitudes. Yet these are to be kept at a distance, as Rogers holds, to insure the complete independence of the individual. He includes other questions to make clear his belief in separation. "Can I be strong enough as a person to be separate from the other?" And again, "Am I secure enough within myself to permit him his separateness?" (p. 53).

In Chapter 1, "This is Me," he speaks of the learnings he has found significant. He notes the value of accepting and understanding another person. "I have found it enriching to open channels whereby others can communicate their feelings, their private perceptual worlds, to me" (p. 19). Yet he declares his independence—"evaluation by others is not a guide for me" (p. 23). And he concludes: "Experience is, for me, the highest authority" (p. 23). No other person's ideas are found to be as authoritative for him as his own experience.

We must respect the honest integrity of Carl Rogers in his decision to be himself. He does confirm the significance of the interpersonal relationship in counseling. Yet his goal for therapy is to free the individual from close involvement with other persons. Let the individual actualize himself by maintaining and enhancing his own organism.[11] This seems to me unreal, confining, encapsulating, and unfulfilling in the largest sense of his potentialities as a social being.

The goal of responsive counseling is to move out of the self-actualizing capsule to the intercreative community. Whatever is learned in the counseling encounter is not to terminate with the lonely individual in self-enhancing independence. The outcome of responsive counseling is to enter more effectively into outgoing and fulfilling relationships with other persons, who become a living community.

[11] *Client-Centered Therapy,* p. 487.

4. How Does the Counselor Respond?

I have proposed responsive counseling as a more accurate description of what the counselor does. His response is a positive activity in contrast to negative passivity implied by nondirective counseling. To respond is to be fully alive and alert, to listen and answer back in reply to one who addresses me. It is by accepting and attentive listening that the person is invited to speak in confidence more freely and fully. The counselor is responsive to every mood, feeling, and attitude expressed. Yet his aim is not to reflect feeling only, but to give himself in a total response to the whole being of the other person.

This is not client-centered but interpersonal counseling. What both are seeking is the open response of person to person in the deep respect we know as I and Thou. This is not permissive listening only, but a dialogue of address and response. This is more than empathy, by which the counselor perceives how the client feels; it is a two-way *tele*[12] or communication back and forth from person to person. This is not verbal exchange only, but existential encounter in the profound responsiveness of interpersonal meeting. The locus of value is not in the client alone as one who must be sufficient to himself, but in the relationship where each person is responsible to the other.

Responsive counseling is a mutual going forward together. We may see this best as a series of steps or "stages on life's way" [13] where we walk together.

[12] "The simplest unit of feeling transmitted from one individual towards another." J. L. Moreno, *Who Shall Survive* (Beacon, N.Y.: Beacon House, 1953), p. 314.

[13] Sören Kierkegaard gives us this phrase to portray his pilgrimage from the aesthetic to the ethical and religious spheres of existence (1845).

1. The person is received and accepted as he is.
2. Mutual responsibility is defined and engaged.
3. The counselor listens deeply and responds to feeling.
4. I meet Thou in the encounter of open dialogue.
5. Together we acknowledge negative feelings and positive impulses of growing insight and action.
6. In facing these dilemmas we jointly explore options of choice and alternative ways of life.
7. The counselor sustains the person in his search for identity from which he can see more clearly who he is and come to basic decisions in his concrete situation.
8. From this searching and growing there will be outgoing steps toward other persons in more trusting and creative relationships.

The counselor participates interpersonally in a responsive mood of dynamic repose. He seeks to relax and be free of haste or agenda anxiety. He yields initiative to the other person, yet sustains him faithfully throughout the painful steps of searching and growing. He asks few questions and rarely gives advice. He respects limits which are to be clearly defined, yet he gives himself fully up to those limits. He is steadily there, wholly present without retreat or pressure.

The counselor is more than a mirror to reflect the feelings and perceptions of the client. He completes the circuit of interview by giving back from his own experience what he receives from the other person. He searches with the person through hidden labyrinths and dark passageways for the moving, dynamic meaning of his life with the persons around him. He sharpens the focus of perception by the interchange of mutual understanding, of insight and foresight. Through perception and practice they seek enlarging fulfillment of all relationships, beginning with this one and going beyond the counseling room to other persons in the living community. When counseling terminates, the person is prepared to move steadily with new understanding and confidence into other significant relationships of his expanding life.

In Tokyo it was my privilege to see an educational film, *Alto of the Spirit,* portraying a depressed person in counseling with Professor Fujio Tomada. As the young woman began to see a path of light in her darkness she sang to him a Christian hymn in a rich alto voice. It occurred to me then that counseling is, in fact, a duet of the spirit, in which the counselor is sustaining the person by his responsive spirit, upholding the melody of his search with the harmony of going forward together.

Recently a counselor, who is also an organist, has given me his view of the counselor as the accompanist who assists the soloist in his artistic communication.

> In the first place, the skilled accompanist accepts the soloist as he is. He accepts his limitations as far as musical ability is concerned. He does try not to alter the performer's concept of a particular musical number, but may ask, "This is the way you want to do it? Do I understand what you want to do here?"
>
> When the soloist sings or plays off pitch the accompanist does not change the key, for this would distort reality. Rather he disregards his own score and reinforces the melody line. He says by his playing, "Here we are, isn't this the pitch you intend?" [14]

He compares group counseling to a symphony orchestra, where each person has his own part to play in response to every other player. A conductor will hold back the whole orchestra while he coaxes a fragile melody from the flute, which otherwise would

[14] Personal conversation with Oliver Francisco, January 5, 1965, in East Longmeadow, Massachusetts.

have been covered. He does not force them to play softly; he helps each one to express himself best in the interplay and harmonic expression of the whole composition. Every person needs a supporting cast to fulfill his purpose as a responsible member of the human society.

In the symphony of life there is discord as well as harmony, as each player searches for the notes to express his part in relation to all who join with him in the community of orchestration to make the most of their lives together. Counseling is a sustaining duet by which to learn how to play one's best in the full orchestra of living relationships.

The person struggles through anxious conflict into the joyful anguish of interpersonal growth. It is not always so easy or decisive as it may seem, when excerpts are selected from interviews, to resolve the counseling. Conflicts are deep, and the anxieties of therapy are very painful. Wanting to defend ourselves from the pain and escape from the struggle, we resist the discipline of counseling. Yet through counseling we find that the wholeness we seek comes only by struggle and discipline.

It is not surprising that we are ambivalent about this counseling. We are always hoping for an easier way and a smoother shortcut to the end of the rainbow. We know this in our lucid moments of truth. We know that the tendency to retreat must be faced honestly and turned into open encounter. No single encounter is enough to prepare for the arduous vocation to which we are called. We must enter more fully into every relationship of human life with growing sensitivity and responsibility. Counseling will end, but growth must go on through self-giving love and open dialogue, where person responds to person in creative fulfillment.

4

A Method of Pastoral Counseling

1. Modifying the Pioneers

It would be folly for the pastoral counselor to start *de novo*, as if he were a new Adam with no precedents or predecessors to follow. The inventive genius is not the one who ignores the work of the past but rather one who builds upon it. The best explorer is the one who studies the maps and marked trails of other travelers, who learns everything he can of terrain, climate, obstacles, hazards, and resources to prepare the better for his journey. He may choose a new course for himself, but only after considering the alternatives and consulting the experience of others who have gone that way.

So as the pastor seeks to develop a method of counseling, he will need to study the methods of other counselors. He will not copy others in exact imitation, for he is a unique person and he must be truly himself in meeting the person before him. He will have much to learn of other professions, yet he must be true to his own distinctive calling as a pastor. He will continue to search for his own personal identity among others who have their different, yet similar, ways of living out their uniquely common life. We honor the pioneers by following them and by differing from them. If we go beyond them it is because they have shown us the way so far.

Among the pioneer counselors of our time we are indebted to psychologists such as Carl Rogers and psychiatrists such as Sigmund Freud. No pastoral counselor can ignore these pioneers who opened the way before us. Yet even as we learn from them we will modify them. The pioneer is controversial, and heated debates will rage violently around him. In the passionate devotion of intense and conflicting loyalties, it may be contended that we must either accept or reject each one *in toto*. But as the dialogue continues and the dust settles, we see the work of all this threshing about is to sift the wheat from the chaff. As time lifts up the permanent from the temporary, those who follow will carry forward what is most significant in the work of each pioneer.

In the pages to follow I hope to show our debt to these pioneers, even as we undertake to modify their theories, sift out what is most essential for us, and press forward a step or more along the way we must choose to go. It is actually the followers of Freud who most insist upon revising his theories, and there is not a shadow of doubt that the work of revision will go on. Rogers invites modification by asking not for orthodox agreement, but for each counselor to offer his own theory of counseling as a hypothesis for testing.

It is clear that a profession like psychiatry, cannot be the model for another vocation such as the pastoral ministry. Each field has its own ground on which to stand and its own boundaries to mark it off from other fields. Each profession, as we have noted in Chapter 1, emerges from a sustaining community with its own history, goals, and terms of reference. The pastor who counsels will therefore stand forth as distinct from the physician or psychologist who functions from another base and context. The leaders in pastoral counseling, such as Seward Hiltner, Carroll Wise, Wayne Oates, André Godin, and Heije Faber, are vigorously modifying the theory of the secular counselors.

In similar vein, the method here presented will work over and modify what we may learn from this interdisciplinary dialogue. What is here called responsive counseling is the outcome of listening and responding to other views and voices. Until we are open to observe and listen, to experience and participate with others in what they are finding, we are not able to be responsive in the profound sense of growing discovery which is counseling.

If the dialogue is true communication, there will be listening and learning from both sides. Pastoral counseling will be modified by this conversation with other disciplines. The pastor may be in a sealed and sterile theological cocoon until he comes out to circulate in the world among other men who see life differently and challenge his dogmatic assumptions. We have equal right to expect that other disciplines will also be modified as they come out of their closed systems and interchange views and experiences with the open-minded pastor. Unless both are open-minded the change will be slight and the learning crippled by retaining walls and confining limits. If even one person is open, however, there is a possibility of awakening the other to see a glimmer of light. And if barriers can be reduced, there is hope of fresh air and new light breaking in to invigorate the search for larger understanding.

Spiritual counseling is the distinctive field of the pastor. He is called to bring a spiritual ministry to the emotional life. This is needed as urgently as any service to human life. For persons in search of identity, meaning, purpose, and values to live by are not fulfilled by any measures that fall short of their spiritual concerns. Viktor Frankl calls this the human dimension,[1] for man is human by virtue of his spirit, by which he decides the central issues of his life and destiny. "Only the height of man is man," as Paracelsus said in his time. Psychotherapy is not enough, as Frankl shows. Therapy is needed for illness, and on this we agree. But for the true center of our lives we need a spiritual awakening and inner decision. Psychotherapy needs to be supplemented and extended by logotherapy, which is spiritual counseling, to seek the meaning of life by finding our responsibility in the concrete situation before us.

The doctor will have his medical ministry to the spirit of man, as Frankl shows in *The Doctor and the Soul.*[2] The surgeon who removes a leg has not completed the job if the patient commits suicide, unable to live as a cripple. It is also the doctor's responsibility to help him find a meaning by which to live. So the pastor has a specific spiritual ministry to enter into suffering, despair, guilt, and doubt with searching and sustaining faith to discover purpose in life and our best response to each situation.

Can the counselor leave decisions entirely to others? Is he not responsible to search with the person and affirm with him the

[1] Frankl, *Man's Search for Meaning: An Introduction to Logotherapy*, tr. by Ilse Lasch (Boston: Beacon Press, [1946], 1963).

[2] Tr. by Richard and Clara Winston (New York: Alfred A. Knopf [1955], 1963).

values by which a sound decision can be made? A leading mountain climber will keep the rope slack to give freedom for each person to do his own climbing. But if there is danger of a fall, he will plant his feet and tug with all his strength. The counselor must know the ground on which he stands, and the kind of relationship that will be dynamic enough in spiritual energy to keep a person from destruction while he is struggling up the way of growth.

How will the pastor proceed to be a spiritual counselor? Seward Hiltner has a clear view of pastoral counseling in theological and psychological perspective.[3] His theological approach is that pastoring is shepherding with concern, acceptance, understanding, clarification, judgment, and patience to stand by persons in every condition of life. His psychological approach is eductive counseling, drawing out of the person his potentialities to cope with the situation.[4] The term is from *educere,* the same root from which "education" is derived. Yet he does not mean teaching by lecturing deductively in authoritarian manner, but assisting the person inductively to develop his insights from within his own experience.

Eduard Thurneysen, Swiss pastor and associate of Karl Barth, sees pastoral care and counseling as proclamation.[5] He distrusts psychology and pietism which hope to find truth within man. The truth is from God in judgment, forgiveness, and grace. The counselor is to be a channel through which the Holy Spirit can speak. He would oppose the subjectivity of Hiltner's eductive counseling with the wholly-other objectivity of God's word to man. This might be seen as a choice between a pastoral theology

[3] *Pastoral Counseling.*
[4] *Ibid.,* pp. 97, 253.
[5] *A Theology of Pastoral Care.*

and a pastoral psychology. But actually the choice is among theologies in their different view of man's destiny as much as it is among psychologies in their contrasting ways of understanding the nature of man. American pastoral counselors like Hiltner are bringing theology and psychology into conjunction as they train the light of one upon the other that each may be illuminated by the other.

Thurneysen does recognize that pastoral care needs psychology as its outstanding auxiliary. "True pastoral counselors have always been true psychologists" (p. 202). We cannot know enough about man; neither can we be expert enough in the methods and perceptions of psychology. But there is no equality in his view between psychology and theology, for psychology is ancillary and phenomenological with no authority to make declarations beyond descriptions of man's inner being (p. 210).

> The true pastoral counselor is always a translator of the Word (p. 202).
>
> We shall really understand man only when we understand him from the Bible. There is disclosed what man is and what no psychology is able to disclose by itself: man's misery and man's greatness (p. 205).
>
> The Word of God is not one source of knowledge among others; it is the basis of all knowledge even in the matter of understanding man (p. 206).

My own approach is responsive counseling, a third mediating way between the eductive approach from within man and the deductive approach of revelation from above. There is danger we may fall into one trap or the other of authoritarian or permissive counseling; and either extreme will undermine effective growth by paralyzing initiative or responsibility. Responsive counseling calls forth both initiative and responsibility by mutual participation in true dialogue. The counselor needs to relax authority enough to participate as a fellow searcher who actively undertakes to learn and grow with the other person. Yet the counselor cannot afford to abdicate his authority if he is to engage the person in direct encounter and awaken his initiative to call forth dormant potentiality. This counseling dialogue explores the meaning of life in our personal-social-spiritual context by responding to the challenge of each situation in the active voice of a person who decides to be responsible.

Responsive counseling will be at once active and receptive. In my seven years with Joseph H. Pratt, M.D., the medical founder of group therapy at the Boston Dispensary, we would begin the group meeting with a period of relaxation; then invite each one to speak of his condition and respond to each other in the group by talking it out and acting upon a growing spiritual faith. Jacob L. Moreno, M.D., another pioneer in group therapy, has developed psychodrama to call forth emotional responses spontaneously, by meeting other persons openly in dramatic encounter and learning through role training to play a responsible part in social participation. Viktor Frankl, M.D., with whom I have worked in Vienna Poliklinic, where he is director of the neurological clinic, offers logotherapy as a direct encounter of person to person, to relax the compulsive and phobic obsessions by paradoxical intention (to welcome what we fear with a sense of humor and a willingness to accept whatever comes with hope and courage), to arouse inner strength of spirit, to search for the meaning of life in the concrete situation, and to meet the demands of life with a new decision to be a freer and more responsible person.

A pastoral counselor is constantly engaged in the interaction of person to person and man to God. He seeks to nourish and deepen the rich meaning of interpersonal relations. He invites open and significant communication in small group fellowship. His primary task is not to cure illness but to promote growth through creative relationship. His counseling will aim to search with the person for his own identity through encounter of spirit with spirit, to decide who he is and what he will seek to become as a participating member of the loving, ministering community. Through such living and dynamic encounters, he will seek to be authentic and outgoing to other persons in growing personal and social responsibility.[6]

In this chapter we will explore the method of responsive counseling in the pastoral context. As we come to focus upon this responsive method of pastoral counseling, we will need to turn from abstract generalizing to specific procedures in concrete situations. It is not accurate to treat counseling as a uniform progression as on a straight and level highway from here to the distant horizon. There are many turnings and ups and downs in the course of human life. There are phases of development to live through, plateaus of inertia and bursts of sudden insight, moments of defeat and loss, baffling frustration and uncertainty; as well as liberating times when there is freedom to grow, to discover the meaning of life, to find an answering response, and to know a deeply satisfying fulfillment.

The counselor will expect these variations in the course of every life. If he is sensitive to changing moods, he will be responsive to each new event from moment to moment. His style of

[6] This approach is clearly delineated in two recent publications from European theologians, one in the Reformed Church of Holland, and the other in the Roman Catholic Church of Belgium: Heije Faber and Ebel van der Schoot, *The Art of Pastoral Conversation* (Nashville: Abingdon Press [1962], 1965); and André Godin, *The Pastor as Counselor.*

counseling will not be set in a rigid pattern or tuned to one key, but alive to many tones and sensitive to the whole range of human emotions. He will perceive that no mood is pure or simple but is rather a constant blending together of many disonant feelings in a rich complexity.

In the course of counseling, which may continue for many months, we can sense a dynamic movement from one stage of development to another. This will vary from person to person, and yet the overall design is rather predictable. The sequences through which an individual develops will tend to recapitulate the phylogenetic development of the species. The growing child will have typical developmental tasks for each age of his growing life. We shall not, therefore, be surprised to find somewhat regular phases through which a person may be expected to move in counseling. Let us consider first the opening phases in pastoral counseling.

2. *The Opening Phases*

The pastor is well prepared in deductive methods of reasoning. Historically, theological education has started with a general principle or dogma from which the whole system of thought and action was deduced. Beginning with the Bible as a revelation of God's acts and intentions in the world, we are shown the condition of man and what is expected of him according to the law and the gospel. When the preacher speaks to his congregation, he is expected to begin with a text, and from this authority to declare the message to which we are called to respond. This deductive reasoning may be a rousing challenge, yet it often has the opposite effect of a depressant, causing resistance from hearers who do not want to be told what to believe or do.

Counseling begins with the person where he is, and proceeds from there by inductive steps to eventual conclusions. A counselor will know from clinical experience and psychological understanding how the pressure of authority naturally calls forth resistance. If the counselor has a ready answer that he hopes will fit, he can hardly wait to show the person, "Here it is! This is what you are looking for." But experience teaches us how little a ready answer can accomplish, for it is external to the person, and consequently not for him; it is not his idea, but rather what the authority imposes upon him, i.e. pressure to be resisted.

"Experience teaches us," we have just said. What a great lesson this is to learn. Actually, there is no way to learn the inner meaning of life but out of our own experience. The best teachers know this, and seek to create live, first-person experiences in which we may learn together. Counseling is this kind of learning and teaching from shared personal experience. Diving into the depths of myself alone provides inward discovery, but it is not the whole experience of learning. We learn best in sharing personal experiences openly and thoughtfully with each other. The verbal learning of words will not do, or observing what others may do, though these are personal experiences too. The full experiencing of all that is our life, freely shared in open communication, invites the utmost learning.

When the pastor is preaching he aims to give the word, but when he is counseling he wants to receive the word. Listening is now a more urgent call for the counselor than speaking. Good listening is not easy, especially for one who is trained to speak. This art of listening is more difficult than the art of speaking. To listen well requires discipline learned by constant training, learning to check the impulse to speak or dominate and control, to change the focus from what I think and want to say to what you feel and struggle to express. In place of searching for words to project on you, I must quietly waken sensitive hearing to perceive what you feel, and thereby come to know what life means to you. It is not easy for us to express what is most deeply felt, and never all at once. So I must learn to be patient in faithful, responsive listening, to catch a glimpse here and a signal there of the hidden feelings which you conceal, yet hope to reveal when the moment of rapport is trusting and open enough to bring forth.

What we need most in the initial phase of counseling is to be open. The opening mood is *relaxation*. We come to counseling out of the tensions of daily life, caught in the dilemmas and tangled in the conflicts which are the source of our human anguish. We are closed in behind our defenses. These are not so much true shields, set to ward off danger, as our very selves in the tensely anxious guarding which is the style of our life. We are contracting the muscles of the eyes and throat, of arms and legs, of respiration and viscera to be ready for whatever danger may suddenly appear. In this readiness for danger, which is the characteristic posture of life in a world of hidden threats, we are not open persons but closed to each other and always on guard.

Freud discovered that when his patients reclined on the couch, they were better able to relax the tensions of body and mind. He further instructed them to relax the fearful control of their thinking, to have the mind open to any thoughts or memories that occurred to them, and to speak openly of whatever came to them no matter how painful or absurd it might be. With this method of free association, as he called it, the person was more at liberty to recall significant experiences into the light of conscious awareness. Repressed feelings came out of hiding into the foreground of attention.

To be open we need to relax these defensive and restrictive contractions of life. The counselor himself must first relax if he is to help the other person relax his anxious, defensive tensions. The pastor prepares for the counseling hour by letting go his driving pace and hurried tempo, putting aside his crowded agenda, and setting his mind free to stretch and expand. Releasing his self-containment and yielding the distance of his cherished privacy, he seeks to be an open person, free to enter wholeheartedly into the counseling relationship. The pastor prepares by praying to God in quiet communion for sight to look at the other person as God may see him in his painful anguish and nascent potential to grow. He asks God to dissolve his rigid prejudices, his unwilling resistance, his pride of authority, and his pet theories into accepting and receptive attitudes of loving concern. Such moments of relaxation before counseling are essential preparation for a true encounter of person with person.

When Mrs. Hilt[7] enters the pastor's study he sees her as a person in distress. Her tired face and drooping form move toward the armchair in a visible mood of hopeless despair. He knows the burdens of life are heavy upon her, and before either one speaks he quietly responds with empathy and concern to bear her burden with her. He accepts her in the security of basic trust which is his religious faith, tested and renewed to rely upon. As she senses this atmosphere of trust and acceptance, she is able to release her anguish and sorrow. Her feelings pour out in a

[7] Personal names are fictitious, but the story is true and used with permission. The conversation is reconstructed from notes taken by the counselor during the interviews.

torrent as she tells of her two daughters in mental hospitals, of her husband who blames her for this, and the hopeless feeling of being trapped with no way out.

Mrs. Hilt 1: I was upset yesterday when our daughter June telephoned at 8:00 A.M. asking for sleeping pills. She is twenty-three years old, a graduate of the university, yet she seems unable to hold a job. She makes errors as if she is asking to fail. Her ideals are high. She wants to be a writer and go on for graduate study. But now she is in a mental hospital, and quite disturbed. She often telephones collect when she is upset, but she does not listen to anyone, and this upsets me too.

Counselor 1: We wonder how to respond to these breathless requests.

H 2: She is dependent on her father, who deals with her gently and tenderly. It is a bone of contention between us that he favors her. I say "no," and then he says "yes." My husband tells me not to cross her but be sweet, and so I try. But I have given up trying to discipline her since high school. I turned her over to him, but I am miserable to have this going on.

C 2: It *is* a helpless feeling to be left out this way.

H 3: Then there is May, who dropped out of school in the eleventh grade. She is more like me, a quitter, not a fighter like her father. She is quiet, gives me no trouble, but is failing in everything and completely apathetic. She was in the state hospital the first time for three months, and they gave much time to her because of her youth, but to no avail. This time she has been in the hospital eight months and does not improve. She comes home every other weekend, but sleeps all the time. We get along fine, but May is a reflection of myself. I have to push to appear ambitious, and she is hopeless, like me, with no meaning for existence. She has negative responses like me, but I snap out of it and she does not.

C 3: Though you try to help her she does not seem strong enough to stand on her own feet.

H 4: It is a burden for me to feel I am the cause of this. If I had put myself out of the picture years ago the girls would be independent. I want to die, but it is too late now. It would be devastating to them. If I could only find out why I want to die. Never could know. It's ridiculous. I must be taking a wrong attitude somewhere. When I get depressed there is nothing to do but wait.

C 4: When you feel that you are the cause of your daughters' troubles, the burden is almost too heavy to bear. Yet wanting to die is not going to help them.

The pastor listens to feel and understand what this sorrow means to her. He listens with the full attention of his whole being to comprehend the intricate complexity of it. Together they search for a truer realization of what life is, under the misery of this distress. The pastor has learned through clinical pastoral training with persons in such distress not to deny the feelings expressed, but to accept them even though they seem negative. To deny the feeling is to separate the counselor from the person in his anguish, to cause estrangement between them and block the progress they may find in going forward together.

There is much to learn in this opening phase from Carl Rogers' nondirective, client-centered therapy. He shows how the most important preparation of the counselor will always be a warmly accepting attitude toward the person. If he stands off to look at her from an external point of view, to diagnose or judge, interpret or generalize, moralize or dogmatize, he separates himself from her. She will then have to defend if he seems to be attacking, and to resist if he seems to be judging or telling her what to do and what to believe.

If the counselor instead of saying, "We wonder how to

respond," had noted how unreasonable the daughter was or how unstable the mother was to be so easily upset, there would be a different tone to the conversation, one of judging and being judged.

If instead of responding to her despair with, "It *is* a helpless feeling," he had said, "You gave her up when you might have been stronger," she would feel the pastor was giving her up because she was weak. Her confession would falter, and feeling rejected, she would return to the isolation of broken communication.

When the counselor holds to the internal frame of reference, as Rogers shows, he is accepting her as she is, without pushing or pulling her to his external position. He may want her to change; but to urge or recommend, to correct or persuade, is to show that he does not accept her at the very time when she most of all needs accepting in the very midst of her faults and shortcomings. Until she can feel accepted and understood, she cannot begin to find confidence enough to withstand the self-rejection of hating herself, or the waves of despair that overwhelm her with impulses to die. Nothing less than complete acceptance will save her from that fatal estrangement, or call her back from death to life.

Yet who can give complete acceptance to the unacceptable person who seems to have failed? The pastor will know in the searching of his own heart that this is most difficult for him who cherishes such high ideals of religious perfection. He devotes himself to upholding these high standards of moral perfection, to declaring them and bringing others to practice them. His mission is to save others from weakness and despair, and his evangelistic zeal impels him to exert every means to persuade and call men to repent and enter a new life. Does this misfit him for the work of a counselor, which is to listen empathically, to wait patiently, to accept the unacceptable, and to have faith in those who have no faith?

Here the pastor needs to learn of the psychologist to understand the dynamics of personality change. Like the fable of the contest between the wind and the sun, it is not the force of external pressure that causes the man to remove his heavy coat, but the warmth of the sun that gives him the feeling he does not need to wrap himself in such defenses. We cannot, after all, deny the power of emotional warmth that comes from a willingness to give complete acceptance.

Is this not the heart of the Christian gospel the pastor represents? Did not Jesus accept the weak and the infirm, the outcast and the sinner with healing, forgiving love? God is portrayed as the Father who runs to embrace the prodigal son. The neighbor is the foreigner who has mercy upon the bleeding man at the roadside. If we find it difficult to love the unlovely with a whole heart, it may be that we are not whole ourselves, but caught in conflict with deep inner impulses holding us in a bondage we dare not let go, and from which we cannot be free.

The opening phase of counseling will fail unless the counselor himself is open to accept the other person genuinely and wholly. He must be with the person, beside him wherever he is, not above him or ahead of him. If the counselor is above, he will be judgmental from his external point of view. If he is pressing ahead, he will lengthen the distance between them until the person feels left behind and left out. Remote control is not what the person wants in counseling, but someone who cares enough to stand by him and walk with him, step by step at his pace. He knows that his defeat is in lonely isolation, and if the counselor is not really with him he would rather be alone with no pretenses of unmet promises.

Returning to Mrs. Hilt we may ask if the counselor is truly beside her. He seems to be in the first two responses, C 1 and C 2, but does he stay with her in the next two responses? He is evidently trying to reflect her feeling, yet in C 3 he wavers from identification with Mrs. Hilt as subject ("Though you try to help her") to judging May from above as object ("She does not seem strong enough to stand on her own feet"). He might better have said, "You want so much to help her that it breaks your heart when she does not respond." Here there is less judging from above and more accurate response to the center of her tragic feeling.

When Mrs. Hilt speaks of her despair in contributing to her daughters' failures, the counselor in C 4 shows genuine and compassionate understanding ("When you feel that you are the cause of your daughters' troubles, the burden is almost too heavy to bear"). But as she reveals her death wishes, he is concerned and intervenes with the warning, "Yet wanting to die is not going to help them." There is reason to be concerned, for she is depressed and evidently struggles with suicidal impulses. She has opened the subject of wanting to die, and he cannot ignore it or repress it as one of those things we do not talk about.

She is quite ambivalent herself about these death wishes, and moves toward the same conclusion that this is not the way to help her daughters. She wants to explore these impulses more searchingly and asks for light on this dark area of her life ("If I could only find out why I want to die"). The counselor responds to the ambivalence, yet with a dogmatic assertion that tends to close the subject instead of keeping it open. A better response might have been, "The burden is so heavy you wonder if there isn't some way out. Is dying the way, or is there a better way?" In this way, the matter is open to explore further as she has asked to do.

How long will these opening phases continue? This will depend upon the nature of the issues presented, the pace at which the counseling moves, the depth explored, and the readiness for growth. The counselor will be aware that the presenting problem may not be the real problem, and time will be needed to develop a relationship of trust, in which the deeper, more painful, and guarded issues may come to open expression. Unless the opening phases are successful, the counseling will probably fail. The counselor can well afford to be patient, relaxed, and responsive to feeling in these important opening phases, where the course is set for open encounter to follow. But he does not dwell in this mood of relaxation forever, or rest content with the internal point of view alone. Life moves on from one developmental task to the next phase of growth.

3. *The Mid Course*

When counseling moves beyond the opening phases there will be new developments to undergo. What may we expect to develop in the ongoing progress of responsive counseling? As we go forward in counseling we find a characteristic growth we may describe as *deep action*. In the opening phases there is genuine acceptance of the other person in all his tangled conflict and with all his thorny problems. With empathy for the person, the counselor identifies with him at the center of his internal frame of reference, and responds to his feelings as sensitively and accurately as he can. If the opening is well fulfilled, there is already a dimension of depth in the relationship. In listening and accepting there is a mood of relaxation that is passive enough to be open and receptive.

Yet the counselor is at the same time responsive to the feelings of the other person. In this responsiveness he is active in giving full attention, listening and comprehending what the person means, entering into his suffering, and living his experience with him. The two meet at the point of the person's deepest concern, in a mutuality of sharing the experience. It is almost as if the two had become one in seeing and feeling the meaning and vitality of life at this moment. There is a mystical immediacy in this moment as the distance and diversity melt into a unity of converging perception.

We say "almost," but the almost unity of perception does not achieve or sustain the utmost unity of complete identity. There are always two persons, at the very least, in counseling. And this is how counseling is more than a solitary meditation. The dynamic significance of counseling arises from the meeting of two persons, each one a unique and different center of life experience, who are open to give and receive honest interchange of meaning from the counterpoise of each to the other. There must be mutual giving as well as mutual receiving if we expect growth to transpire. Consequently, the outcome of counseling will emerge from the phase of action and self-giving, as much as it will from the passive phase of receiving and introcepting new life.

Deep action has two dimensions which may be called inner action and interaction. Inner action is what goes on within a person; interaction is what goes on between persons. Though we distinguish these two actions for logical analysis, actually they are inseparable. Growth and maturation occur within the person, yet only by interaction with the environment, as in breathing, receiving nourishment, and responding to stimuli. Insight is self-understanding, but it is often more significant when it arises from the mutual searching of an inter-view.

When we speak of depth psychology we usually refer to the deeper emotional life whose dynamic motivations may be hidden in the mystery of the individual unconscious. Yet the most vivid emotions and dreams are in reference to other persons who engage us in the adventures of life. Carl Jung finds rich symbols and meanings in the collective unconscious to which the individual is open and in which he participates with other persons. There are dimensions of depth between persons as well as within the person.

The deep action of counseling is a meeting of persons at the center of their beings. It is not the external appearance which captures attention or the superficial observation of a passing stranger. It is rather the deepening understanding that comes of open dialogue and empathic response to the feelings of another person. We have noted how one person may identify with another through shared experience, until the two converge into one unified perception. There is depth here, and yet as each is true to his own identity, he will assert the unique differences of his own personhood. In the opening phases we each move toward a common center of concern to comprehend what life means to the other. Yet, the more carefully we explore our precise meanings, the more sharply we sense our essential differences. Instead of a circle around one focus, counseling becomes an ellipse around two foci. Instead of reducing our differences as in the opening phase, we move on to heighten the opposition of two persons meeting face-to-face with appropriate distance between them.

The first phase of counseling is acceptance, but eventually the time comes for confrontation. Otherwise, the force of the encounter is reduced to insincere agreeableness. Differences may be smoothed over, individuality is blurred, and true feelings are repressed to give the surface appearance of unanimity. But there is a hollow ring about this surface agreement. It lacks a genuine expression of hidden feelings so repressed as to deny the reality in favor of false sameness. The channel of communication is narrowed until conversation becomes a deceptive meeting on trivial inconsequentials which appear safe, while avoiding the issues that concern us most. Conventional social life is often like this, empty and hollow, to be safe and to avoid revealing oneself or disturbing another. As my father once said in a moment of perceptive honesty, "What we care about the most we talk about the least."

If counseling is to move into the midstream of growing life, we will need to face each other in real encounter. This is what we miss in the nondirective approach. The permissive relaxation of total acceptance is a good way to begin in the opening phase of forming a trusting relationship. But then comes a time to go beyond the client-centered, internal frame of reference, into the open encounter of two strong persons standing face-to-face. The counselor is surely with the person as intensely as before, yet now in challenge as well as support. Once, the counselor stood beside the person in self-effacing unity, now they will stand facing each other as the counselor manifests his own position. Honesty requires it. In such a confrontation we will know the tension of creative opposition. This is the heart of open dialogue: self-revelation and mutual response.

When the counseling began with Mrs. Hilt, she was lost in identification with her daughters. She talked of them more than of herself; she was in them, and they were in her. She rebelled in their rebellion; she suffered in their sufferings and felt hopeless in their apathy and despair. The counselor gave her support by entering into her distress and bearing the emotional burden with her. But farther along, in another interview, they turned to face each other with a new sense of unique differences and the distance that separated them, each to stand on his own ground over against the other. She now presents herself in a new light as a person searching for her own identity.

H 5: It helps to talk. We were discussing others but not getting down to me. I am still waiting for someone to listen to me. Talking to my pastor [not this counselor], I am trying to get a new image of myself, and I do not like to dig up from the past what might soil this image. I busily try to forget. Now I try to think who I am, and it is painful.

C 5: We may fear the shadow we are hiding, and yet we need to know who we are.

H 6: My life is a long series of unrequited loves. I was a lonely child. Father married at forty-five and never showed affection; kissing was unsanitary. Father was reserved and mother was melodramatic. She was twenty years younger and there was tension at home. He was wrapped up in business. She had been a schoolteacher and was always at the store helping. She had no time for me; we avoided each other. My parents doted on my brother four years older. He was brilliant and talented, and he died at eighteen of polio.

C 6: We can have different feelings about death, and how it may affect our family life.

H 7: I was an accident, a girl my mother did not want. I was always a disappointment to my parents. They thought I had poor judgment and my brother had good judgment. I was hopeless because they left me alone. I would tell myself, "Don't you hope for this, and you will not be disappointed."

C 7: Yet isn't one disappointed anyway? Living without hope may be a hopeless way of living.

H 8: Yes, it was.

C 8: Without love, life would be very empty indeed.

H 9: When I was fourteen I became attached to John, who lived across the street. He was fifteen years older, and older men attracted me. My brother opposed him and said I could never do anything with him, but I stood up for him. . . . He was the kind of person I wanted to be. He had left the church never to return, but he had his own religion. I identified with him as my ideal, the main interest in my life. I did not go around with boys or girls my own age, I was so occupied with him. He has always done my thinking for me. He said I was to marry him, and I did it for him.

C 9: Seeking to replace the lost brother who died, and the father and mother who deserted you.

H 10: I have never respected myself because others are always making my decisions and I feel inferior to every one. I turned to him, and he has kept me dependent on him ever since. . . . I can't remember the happy times. There must have been some; he says I just can't remember. It was an early sex awakening but not fulfilling. He said, "What do you expect, fireworks in sex?" as if I expected too much. Sex is not what I want, but a closer feeling with him, companionship with him, in mutual respect as human beings.

C 10: Companionship and respect of person for person most of all.

H 11: He lives as if he were still a bachelor. When he comes home he goes to his room and locks the door. This hurts, but he needs a great deal of privacy. When he goes to bed he locks the door. He does not share life with me as an equal, but treats me as a child. He does not permit me to drive the car. He keeps the money and does all the shopping by himself. He says I am incompetent. My husband has always regarded me as a weakling. I have become resigned and submissive. Seeing the effect on the girls, I don't raise my voice.

C 11: With no ground to stand on we may submit. But still we seek to fulfill an empty existence.

H 12: Why am I so miserable? I am terrified that I could not stand on my own feet. New Year's Day at 10:00 P.M. I went to my room, locked the door, and at long last had a cigarette. For months I had been trying to give it up, but I felt my whole life depended upon this slender white cylinder. All day I had been out hiking. John took me out to dinner. I hate myself and I hate them. I had a feeling blood would run that night if I did not find relief. So, I smoked a cigarette. I prayed, "No human being can help me; God will you help me?" Then I went to sleep. But how many times can I go through this?

Bringing these experiences to the counselor she begins to unload the burden. Holding the anguish out to him, she is not so overwhelmed by it, for it is there between them where they can see it more clearly and objectively. In telling the story, she has already related the past with the present and sensed the continuity of events that may reveal cause and effect. She is not so crushed by the closeness of these terrifying emotions, as they are openly and honestly communicated to the counselor. By looking at life with her, the counselor is already broadening her vision to see it in larger perspective. These difficulties have been a long time in the making. They cannot be undone in a swift blow. The goal of counseling is growth—out of the entangling past into the new being she wants to become.

While the counselor is patiently listening to Mrs. Hilt, he is not passive. He is profoundly moved by the suffering and despair that overflows her. He responds with open awareness to see and understand what these experiences mean to her. He offers his willingness to stand in her place and bear with her the anguish of her distress. And yet he is not stationary or immobile. There is within him a stirring of deep concern for her plight, with active responses of empathy, mutual distress, and perceptive discernment of her condition.

He searches with her for the meaning of these experiences. He traces the interacting dynamics of family life, with her parents and brother, then with her husband and daughters, to see what each is expecting of the other, how each reacts to and against the other. The oldest daughter is seen as defiant of the mother yet dependent upon the father, playing one parent against the other in rivalry for affection, father and daughter in league against the mother. The younger daughter is too much like her mother in moods of apathy and helpless despair, with no hope in living, no interest in school or family or friends, giving up everything, and wanting only death.

The counselor accepts these sorrows as his own, but he does not give up hope or yield to despair. He has faith in the power of spirit to rise above despair. He knows the faithful, sustaining presence of God, the inner peace and strength of new life flowing into moments of weakness. He meets her fear with undaunted trust, and her anger with a love that is ready to forgive the hurt. He offers the healing of God's love to create her a new person. As the session draws to a close they enter into the act of prayer, offering to God the fears and the hope of new life, thanking him for a chance to start again with growing courage to give this new life to the family from hour to hour.

As we review the conversation of Mrs. Hilt and the counselor, we see them moving from the opening phase of relaxation to the middle phase of deep action. She affirms, in H 5, the freedom she finds in talking out her feelings. With new freedom she turns the focus upon herself as a person in her own right, and asks the counselor to help her, even though it causes her pain, to see herself more clearly. In C 5, he acknowledges that what she is hiding needs to come into the open, so that she may know who she is.

She then brings forth her unfulfilled need for love, her rivalry with her deceased brother, and her failure to win the affection of her parents. Perhaps the counselor is fearful that she is asking him for love; at any rate he skirts around love, in C 6, to fasten upon the death of her brother and how this has affected her ("We can have different feelings about death"). He seems to sense her ambivalent feeling toward her brother's death; if she welcomed his going away to end the unhappy rivalry and gain the parents' affection for herself, she would also suffer guilt and terror in this fatal event.

But she reveals that the situation did not improve after the brother's death; her losses were even harder to bear; they left her alone; and she gave up hoping for love. The counselor, in C 7, points up the lesson of this experience in saying, "Yet isn't one disappointed anyway?" There is a sharp thrust here to contend with her helpless resignation. He risks the danger that she may feel separated by his thrusting question. And he softens the blow by reflecting her feeling, yet it is also a lesson to ponder whether hopelessness can ever be a way out of despair ("Living without hope may be a hopeless way of living"). His choice of the verb "may be" avoids dogmatic assertion and invites her to decide from her own experience the outcome of this mood.

She agrees, in H 8, but without developing the idea. The brevity of her response suggests a pause and lost momentum. This could be a dead end, and yet the pause may be a creative moment for both of them. It is not to be broken into hastily to keep the blessed sound flowing at any cost. There is deep action in these moments of silence to bring about quiet awareness. The counselor does not want to change the subject and lose the continuity of the developing experience before it matures. Seeing a relation between hopelessness and lovelessness, he picks up the theme of love which he had previously overlooked and responds to her central concern as the insight dawns more clearly ("Without love, life would be very empty indeed"). If he had once feared to confront the urgency of her quest for love, there may now be a maturing in him of openness to love. Can he let love come into the counseling without distorting the purity of their relationship? Yet he does affirm from his own experience what she has found to be the central motive of any life worth living. In this meeting of experience from two very different persons there is a truer understanding of life.

From this mutual insight she is able to relive her lifelong quest for love. Denied this love at home she turns at fourteen to John, fifteen years older, with whom she identifies, as her ideal. There are so many facets to this experience, the counselor wonders which one to select for emphasis. He is impressed by her revelation, "Older men attracted me," and notes the struggle with her older brother who opposes John. It was this brother who had "good judgment" and was favored by their parents, but who died in the very same year. Drawing these observations together, the counselor responds, in C 9, with a significant insight, "Seeking to replace the lost brother who died, and the father and mother who deserted you."

But she seems not to have heard him, which indicates it was his insight not hers, significant to him but extraneous to her, because she was in pursuit of another discovery, and not ready to consider what the counselor offered her out of his own personal interest. He was that far out of touch with the center of her interest, though he was at one edge of the stream. If he had been in midstream with her, he would have responded less to her family and more to her new love at this moment. He might then have responded, "He was the main interest in your life, and you surrendered completely to him." For she had given up the friends her own age as well as her family for him. She had even given up her own identity, to be John instead of herself, as she said, "He has always done my thinking for me. He said I was to marry him, and I did it for him."

She thought she was surrendering to him for love, but though awakened she was not fulfilled. He possessed her but it was a bondage to reduce her value, rather than a freedom to become more fully herself with him. The emptiness was not filled; at least it was not filled with the love she had hoped for, but with a bitter experience of hatred. She came to hate herself for this surrender that made him everything and herself nothing. Reliving this now was a deep action moving toward the insight to comprehend how great was the loss of her personhood. In H 10, she says, "I have never respected myself because others are always making my decisions and I feel inferior to everyone. I turned to him and he has kept me dependent on him ever since." The counselor comprehends this loss with her as he participates in this deeper searching. His next response confirms this discovery of what the love she seeks must mean to her, something greater and more personal than sex. In C 10, he is in midstream when he says, "Companionship and respect of person for person most of all."

This is what she misses above all. She does not seem to count as a person to John. They live in the same house, yet worlds apart, as he locks himself in his room and locks her out. She finds herself in his eyes a weakling who is incompetent to drive a car, to handle money, or to shop for groceries. After years of struggle, the losses overbalance the gains, and nothing is left but to be resigned and submissive.

The counselor accepts her feelings of submission, but he does not agree to them. He senses in the very midst of her submission a desperate counterthrust to resist the degradation of herself to a nonentity. Lacking in faith and confidence, beset by doubts and hopeless despair, yet she rises deep within to protest, to yearn for respecting love, and to reach out for a new life. Sensing this, the counselor sees the time has come for a confrontation of his vision and faith to meet and challenge her faltering yet striving spirit. It is not the time for a sermon on the courage to be herself, neither is it the time for an extended psychological interpretation. The confrontation must be terse and to the point; it must be personal yet universal; it must be a word for the moment; yet more than a word, it must be a person-to-person encounter as I and Thou.

The counselor confronts her, in C 11, with both sides of her ambivalent feelings, to counter one side against the other. He acknowledges the dilemma and struggles in the midst of it with her, accepting the thrust of her despair and responding with the counterthrust of his dynamic faith. Speaking for himself, he aims also to speak for her, to be her voice as well as his own, to give his strength to oppose her submission. As pastoral counselor he does not do this of himself alone, he represents the Spirit that wrestles with us in our difficulty, that will not give us up, until, like Jacob we are touched and empowered by the creative divinity of that Spirit. What he says is not the whole truth, but simply a growing edge of truth to mount as a wave and ride into the future of enlarging truth. It may seem a simple and fragmentary utterance; yet emerging from the profound conviction of his earnest devotion, in the vivid awareness of this moment, there is something moving here in the deep interaction of the encounter. What the counselor says is at once resignation and determination not to submit, but to answer back with courage, to press on in spite of everything. He is giving a declaration of faith in the most elementary terms for them both: "With no ground to stand on we may submit. But still we seek to fulfill an empty existence."

The counselor was heard, and the message was received. His challenge released from her, in H 12, a flood of anguished searching ("Why am I so miserable?"). Passionately she relives the deep emotional discovery they have shared ("I am terrified that I could not stand on my own feet"). Then she reveals a deep inner action in her that came to a climax on New Year's Day, when she retired to her room, hating herself and hating her family. The intensity of the struggle was very acute, and she knew not whether she wanted to live or die. Then she turned from the slender reeds of man to the ultimate greatness of God, in a prayer of tortured, yet final, thrust: "No human being can help me; God will you help me?" The answering response came to her as a new sense of peace, and she moved from the struggle to refreshing sleep. Even in sleep the deep action will continue to work in the dynamics of the unconscious.

4. The Concluding Phases

It is not easy to recognize where the concluding phases of counseling begin. For each phase in the course of counseling emerges out of the past and moves into the future as a flowing stream. The warm acceptance of the opening phase is already a responsive interaction leading to the deep action of the middle phases. The deep action of the mid-course is an inner growth that may not be visible to the eye, yet it is this hidden growth that leads to the concluding phases. Personal growth is the goal of counseling, and there will be signs of inner growth which become increasingly evident to the person and the counselor. These stages of growth will be recognized and explored in the context of current events and relationships to other persons. As the person comes to see more clearly what he is doing and why he responds as he does, he is freer to change and modify his behavior. He can deal with himself more openly and cope with human situations more responsibly.

Out of such counseling, the person will set his goals more intentionally in reference to the values and purposes of his whole life. He will come to see himself more truly as he is and know where he stands in reference to his goals. Instead of reacting impulsively to a baffling situation or striking out blindly to escape the pressures, he will take a new look at himself and ask, "Why am I doing this? What is it I really want most of all?" Instead of fuming in anger or holding himself in a frozen resentment, he will begin to ask, "What is expected of me? How can I be a responsible person in this situation?" Through pastoral counseling he will find that he does not have to react automatically to stimuli in mechanically determined reflexes. He comes to know himself as a spirit who is able to select stimuli and decide how he will respond. He is more free than he once was, to choose the course of his life, more willing to unify his desires, and more able to carry out his true intentions.

There is much to do in the concluding phases of responsive counseling which we may call *integration*. The person coming to a pastoral counselor is seeking spiritual growth. Whatever the presenting problem may be, whatever the immediate anxiety and special distress, his ultimate concern is the spiritual life. This is why he comes to a pastor, however he may state his case. In some ways his spiritual life is in difficulty, and somehow he seeks personal fulfillment. Otherwise he would go to another counselor and follow another course to the goal he is seeking. He may be asking many things, he may even be confused at the moment in what he is asking, yet beyond each local want there is the ultimate concern of his spirit for something greater than any other need. He is reaching for a truer perspective in which to know himself, a larger context in which to find his place, a destination to guide his destiny each step of the way forever.

What does a pastoral counselor mean to him? From the first impulse to come to a pastor, he will have many contradictory impressions. He will see the pastor as a man of God, called and committed to a religious life centering in the creative spirit he worships, and to whom he is responsible. He will see him as a man of faith who believes that life has meaning and purpose which it is important to know and consider in daily life. He will recognize him to be a man of the church seeking the fellowship of a loving community to care for each and minister to all.

The pastor may be seen as a man who is not quite at home in the world, set apart and encircled by the faithful where he leads a sheltered life. He may be seen as a puritan who is caught within a strict moral code, seeking a perfection not of this world, unable to see or hear evil, and not prepared to accept or understand the temptations of the flesh or the lures of the world, where it is every man for himself and the devil take the hindmost. If the person has this image of the pastor, he may be cautious to speak frankly of his own sins, until he knows the pastor can accept and understand him in his human predicament, go with him through the hell of mortal temptation, bear his burden of guilt with him, open a way of forgiveness for the worst offender and the hope of salvation for the most despairing.

As the counseling proceeds he may learn that the pastor is a very human fellow in spite of the authority vested in him. He may prove to be a good listener with attentive ear to hear the undertones of feeling. He may display a generous spirit to uphold and not bear down or judge hastily, a heart to understand instantly and intuitively. He may not be so stern and unbending as he seemed at first, but may have a rippling sense of humor or a twinkle in his eye to enjoy the adventures of life. He may have the humility to admit he does not know all the answers, yet the willingness to search, the courage to stand for his convictions, and the discerning sense of what, after all, is most significant. He may trust the person even while he is ensnared in the toils of tangled conflict, helpless to see a solution and mired in hopeless despair. He may go along, step by step, until the light begins to dawn, the clouds of despair lift, a better way appears and the goal ahead can be seen, and there is new life and courage to move in the chosen direction.

The person has contradictory feelings about himself too. From mood to mood the contrasts are disturbing, wanting now this and now that, until he wonders which is he and where is the center of his being. From moment to moment the changes of experience are kaleidoscopic, and the efforts to reach many goals are like shadowboxing. He asks himself many questions: Who am I and what do I seek to become? Where do I stand in my family and work group, what do I mean to them, and what do they expect of me? Am I going anywhere with all this striving and these spasmodic bursts of speed, or am I just going around in larger circles that lead nowhere but back to the starting point? What does the counselor really think of me, and how do I feel about my relationship to him? Shall I continue counseling, are we getting anywhere, or have we now come to the goal I was seeking?

The torrent of these vividly contrasting experiences sweeps over the person in counseling. At one moment he is overwhelmed in the flood, another time he keeps his head well above the rushing stream to see where he is going. Little by little the fragments of meaning come together in a design we can comprehend. When midstream is reached, the head is more often above the water, and the perspective is becoming clearer. Moving toward the concluding phases, the many impressions take form and the structure is good to behold. He begins to feel steadier as he sees the structure of life stand forth, and the parts fit together in unified wholeness. He moves ahead more steadily also, as he chooses the main goals he seeks and takes regular steps in their direction.

In the early phases we talk of this and that as if they were unrelated to each other. But then we see the connections that were hidden before, and we hold them together in rising clarity. In this work of integration, persons come more surely into relation to each other. Events that just happened before are now consequential, as we trace the lines of dynamic cause and effect. The lonely isolation of one person fighting against the world gives way to the companionship of persons standing together, counting upon each other, forgiving the hurts and costly mistakes, taking the initiative in reconciling other persons, listening more deeply to hear how they really feel and making a common, yet richly diversified, unity of life together.

Mrs. Hilt came to a pastoral counselor out of her desperate need for spiritual growth. She had known for years that life was going badly, and she could not tolerate the acute sense of failure and helpless inadequacy. A crisis came in a hospital clinic where she was shown how unhealthy emotions were affecting her diabetic condition. She wrote the story as follows:

> This threw me into a fearful spin and I went to the hospital chapel to pray, met the chaplain there and asked him for "something for fear." After a talk and prayer with him, I was able to collect myself and come home by bus unaided, with a new sense of strength, hope, calm. It worked. I wanted more of the same, I knew I was on the right track. God was with me.

She then came for counseling to a pastor near her home. For six months she counseled with him for one hour each week, finding acceptance, understanding, and courage to grow. From him she caught the spirit of the church as a loving community. Since joining the church she has been faithful in attendance, along with her youngest daughter, and appreciates the small group meeting each week for Bible study, prayer, and deepening interpersonal relationships. As the counseling progressed she was able to go more deeply into the events and emotions through which she had suffered so acutely. Reliving these experiences with the counselor, she was better able to cope with them. In the Bible study, prayer, and open conversation about the fears and guilts which so oppressed her, she gathered new strength, faith, and spiritual resources for the challenge of family life.

In the concluding phases the counseling was bringing the crosscurrents and counterforces of her life into growing integration. Significant events were reexamined in the new perspective. Tangled feelings were sifted out and conflicting impulses brought into steadier control. She was learning how to make wise choices and hold to them under stress. She was testing out her insights in the daily round of work and rest, and meeting each person in family and neighborhood in more open encounter. She turned gradually from the moods of self-pity and blame, to hope and faith. She did not wait so much to be loved, with anxious feelings sensitive to slights, but instead, sought ways to show her love and appreciation for her husband and daughters. Finding it possible to move in this direction with new spiritual resources, she was not so crushed and hopeless when something did go wrong. She could let it happen to her without falling apart, by standing her ground and giving her best in a responsible desire to help wherever she could.

The counselor continues to encourage her with interest in every significant detail of her struggle to grow. He has realistic expectations that she cannot leap instantly into a perfect state of heavenly bliss with problems solved once for all. He knows there will be frustrations and disappointments to meet; and he realizes she will make mistakes, suffer anguish, and sometimes fall. But he is helping her learn how to pick herself up after a fall and recover from a mistake without giving up in despair. He knows how much growing is yet needed and how weak she often feels. Yet he also knows of spiritual resources in prayer and communion, in faith and love, which will keep her growing in grace and capacity to meet what life asks. He is more the educator in these concluding phases. He continues to listen and to respond to feeling, but now he is moving more freely in the open dialogue of two-way communication.

H 13: News has come that June is coming home from the mental health center to prepare for graduate study at the university. This will be a test of how to keep her steady and not be upset. She will make demands, and we will have to say no. It is going to be difficult, and she is bringing all her belongings home with her.

C 13: This will be a test of your spiritual growth. And there will be need to forgive.

H 14: This comes easier for me than John, who never forgets an injury. He is an unyielding wall. He says he forgives, but he does not really. The children have the attitude, "you owe me something," and not giving a share back. June's telephone calls are always collect. I would like to tell her off, but my husband will not let me.

C 14: Repressing hostility brings fatigue and illness.

H 15: Since June has been sick I feel guilty to have done this to my girls, so I keep quiet.

C 15: You need to clean out these feelings and be free toward them.

H 16: If I try to talk he calls it nonsense. "Keep quiet." But I still need to be at peace with him and the children. I build a little fence around myself. Then I open the door a little, but when they come in they upset me. I am fearful. To have a little sweet is harder than a strict diet. Divorce is out of the question—too late.

C 16: But how about a spiritual solution? Free and full forgiveness, renewed in prayer and faith.

H 17: Patience is the thing I need.

C 17: This stress comes of tension in defending yourself. Isn't it better to be willing to be hurt, and give yourself fully and openly to them?

H 18: I am not a self-starter. I need the church and prayer and faith. I have tried.

C 18: It is well to know this, and to keep up the means of faithfulness.

H 19: I have tried without success. The tired voice and hopeless feeling spread to others. I should get up earlier to get started right, but I am not a self-starter. My husband's religion and philosophy is inherent in himself. He wants privacy, but I need a group, and

resources like a church. As a boy he had no one to guide him, so he had to be self-reliant.
C 19: What he needs from you is supportive love; this will make a difference. And so with June, to believe in her, potentially.
H 20: I know how much this would mean to me, so I would like to give it to her. But I wake up depressed and tired.
C 20: Can you begin with prayer and verses before getting out of bed to restore the spiritual energies, so the spirit can rise above the drag of fatigue and respond to the challenge? . . .
H 21: [At the close of hour] You have really changed my viewpoint, so I look forward to June's coming, to meet the test and give my best.
C 21: If you can find spiritual resources to bring supportive love at home, it will mean more than we know to enable them to believe and find new life.

O God, thou knowest how deep are the waters, and how long we have been in the crossing. Thou art here and ready to open a new way of life. Bless each member of this family in thy love. Amen.

In this concluding phase the tempo of conversation increases to a more rapid interchange of views. The counselor is listening and responding, teaching and sharing from his experience a way of spiritual growth. It may be that he presses on too urgently, and there is need to sense the resistance or readiness of the person to move at this pace. He is more the pastor guiding her quest for spiritual growth to meet new demands upon her. He leads in prayer and integrates the counseling with worship, sensing her desire for larger faith, and her expectancy that from God will come the new resources by which to rise to the full height of her growing spirit. This seems natural and appropriate where the counselor is also leading the public worship and guiding the congregation in which she participates.

When counseling sessions terminate, the pastoral counselor does not close the case and write "finis" on the last page. If the counselee is in his church the individual counseling moves out into the broadening relationships of the ongoing religious community. There will be frequent contacts at church services and the Bible study group. There may be letters and conversations to communicate in areas of special concern. Most deeply, however, they will be related, through the church, to God and the fellowship of those who seek to grow and to serve in the discipline of faithful disciples who together follow Christ.

Excerpts from her diary and letters give some glimpses of how Mrs. Hilt was meeting the strenuous tests she was facing at home. These will be added to the record of her struggle for spiritual growth.

Jan. 14. Sunny, cold but a *good* day for me. Finally putting to *work* some of the counsel so soundly given me. Putting my mind and house in order for all our sakes, including the pussy cats and the bunny rabbit. Read Bible: "Forgive as we forgive" . . . "but we glory in tribulation also: knowing that *tribulation* worketh *patience;* and patience, *experience;* and experience, *hope* (Romans 5:3-4).

Writing to the counselor the same day, she was seeing her daughter June in a new light.

Right now I am, primarily, psychologically preparing myself for June's homecoming from the mental health center; and incidentally cleaning the whole house, etc. The dread of her arrival has gone as I busily apply myself to thinking of her needs, comforts and appreciating her value as a person, now and potentially (putting to work your counsel). You know, I was so blind before! I took the liberty of reading some of her writings (stored here) and discovered not just a "budding" juvenile author, but a very *good,* fairly adult one, to be respected and highly commended. . . . To me, it is worthy.

Returning to the diary, we read:

Jan. 17. Blizzard. Bitterly cold. . . . Had to get organized early, prepare hearty breakfast for John and get him going (he was tired and late rising) to pick up his daughter plus her paraphernalia. This was harmoniously accomplished by noon. . . . House, dishes, Sunday dinner to prepare. I did it with flourishes and planned it *late* as they are always late. They came in time and everything was *wonderful.* Such *fun* to see June again and note improvement. Hugs and kisses all round. Much cheerful appreciation of the feast, laughter, good feeling. Jan [third daughter] "showed off" amusingly. All got to bed early, considerably fatigued. Unaccustomed joy can be exhausting too, I guess. . . . John requested I make an appointment for a tooth extraction tomorrow.

Jan. 18. I try to get myself going early—insulin, etc. 1½ hours too early. Upsets my schedule. Struggling with insulin reactions, nerves, food, all day. *Managed,* despite above, rather well until noon. *Had* to nap awhile. June's additional laundry, mending, etc., rather overwhelming. I extend myself to the utmost, exhaust my energies, sleep—start over. But no tears or ill feeling. Relationships stand firm and remain loving. Expect and get very little help from other family members. Each has his own duties a-plenty. Boxes and boxes of June's things, John brings in from the car. Remnants of her apartment dwelling, pictures, books, clothes, bedding. I try to look upon it all as "enrichment of the household," instead of pesky hindrance to my own routine. Cooperate with her in taking care of her things. . . .

My mind goes blank, eyesight dims, energies flag and I go to bed at midday exhausted. Wake to get another meal, welcome husband home from dentist—put up his lunch-box—off to work. Try to make him feel appreciated and sympathizing with his having to work after being woozy with novocain (tooth extracted).

When Mrs. Hilt came for pastoral counseling she was trapped and desperately seeking a way out. In counseling she saw that the way out was not to cut herself off from the relationships that distress her. This would have been a step toward death, and she was sorely tempted to take that step in suicide. Nor was she to seek to escape her family by divorce or sudden flight to start a new life. This would have stripped her of all that had most meaning for her. She would have been more empty and forlorn than ever.

Instead of fleeing she has remained within the family relationships that cause her so much anguish. Not believing in herself, she had surrendered her right to be a person and yielded the contest in weak submission. She had been so hurt that she was defending herself with whatever strength she had, withdrawing from the family far enough to hold up a wall between them. This required most of her energy in negative resistance to hold up her own defenses. But now in counseling she came out from her wall of defense to meet each member of the family in the open. This opened her to hurt, but more importantly, to love. Instead of waiting for love to come to her, she now goes forth to give love to others.

Counseling is a way of seeing, a way of seeing what was blurred and cloudy because it was distorted by fear, hostility, guilt, and hopeless despair. It is looking within oneself to see more deeply who she is, and looking out to see other persons more openly and truly. To bring the emotional burden to a counselor who listens, understands, and responds is a prologue to seeing life more clearly in larger perspective.

But seeing is not enough. A person must somehow come into new being. Mrs. Hilt was trapped until she found a glimmer of faith. Out of the depths she cried for a life greater than her own hopeless despair. In this crucial moment she groped her way to a hospital chapel to pray and remained to talk with someone who cared. She gathered new strength to make her way home and go to a pastor for counseling. In the regular hour of counseling each week she saw her need of the church. And in the searching for light she found insight to know herself more deeply, and not only her weakness but also her hidden potentialities, and the pathway to a new and growing life.

From seeing she moved toward being. She was willing to stand on her own feet because she knew she was not alone, willing to step forward into a path of decision because someone was there to meet her. She was able to grow in faith and love and acceptance as she knew she was accepted. She was reaching out in a new spirit of hope and confidence that was communicated to her family. And they were able to accept her forgiving love, her self-giving service because she came to them in a new spirit. She was becoming a new being. She was being now what at first she was only dimly seeing. This was not achieved by one person alone, but in the open dialogue of responsive counseling.

I do not claim that responsive counseling is a panacea for every human ill. There will be limits to what we accomplish by any method. But we do see our lives as engagements with other persons in which we profoundly influence each other. We fall into patterns of conflict to win for ourselves what we fear others are denying or taking away from us. We try to protect ourselves from hurt in defensive ways that isolate us in fear or block communication in anger and resistance.

What responsive counseling seeks is open communication

between two or more persons, each listening and responding openly to the other to know what the other feels, and to care what life means to him. Often there are blocks against God, the creative love flowing to us in spite of our resistance. The pastoral counselor seeks with the person to clear these channels of communication, so life may be renewed and free to experience creative love.

Integration is possible where persons are open to one another, where each one is free to hear and to speak from the heart, to know himself and the other more truly and acceptingly. To respond from this self-knowledge with wisdom of life in truer perspective is to integrate my own conflicting impulses and desires, outgoing to the other person in mutual respect and trusting response-ability. Mrs. Hilt found no instant magic solution to her emotional distress, but she did confess what she had not been able to tell before, and met the grace of a forgiving spirit. She did explore her hidden motives and the inner conflicts which had immobilized her. She began to find the power of the spirit to cope with her losses and rise from despair to a new life. She was learning, even through her mistakes, the need of trust and a willingness to give her best to those who hurt her.

Responsive counseling is a ministry to the emotional needs of persons who seek to grow in spirit. A responsive pastoral counselor is one who trusts the Creative Spirit never to forsake us; and responds to other persons from the creative initiative of this Spirit; open to receive and to give understanding, forgiving, renewing love. Such a counselor does not stand alone. He is open to a Spirit greater than his own, and he works through a ministering community of persons who care for one another in the joy and compassion of One who shows us life in all its fullness.

5
Search for Wholeness

1. Lonely Persons

Health is wholeness. This is a universal goal of all life. For every living creature seeks to be whole.

Mental health is the growing fulfillment of the person, through all the relationships of his life. No one is absolutely complete in a final sense. Health is not a goal line to cross beyond which we can rest forever. It is a fleeting goal that ever moves ahead to beckon us on. The search for health and wholeness is to be renewed each day.

The health we seek is a delicate balance of dynamic relationships within and between persons. The human organism is composed of countless cells and organs sustaining one another in responses of intricate interdependence. We have noted before that no organism can be self-sustaining, but lives only by constant interchange of supplies with the world around. In this interchange of life with life, the counterbalance of the outer world is as urgent as the harmony of the inner world. The growing fulfillment of mental health is a balance of these inner personal and interpersonal relationships.

Mental illness is loneliness. There are many ways of describing and classifying mental diseases. There will be organic and constitutional factors, but they are not the whole story. What is often more disturbing and crucial are the psychosocial conditions. Mental illness for the majority of sufferers is not brain damage but distress in relation to other persons. One is so hurt that he withdraws from active participation with others. He feels rejected, unwanted, and unloved. He is anxious, suspicious, and angry toward others. He cuts himself off and holds up defenses to protect himself from these hurting relations. He is confused and unable to be himself in relation to others with whom he feels insecure. He is blocked from open communication with other persons. His need for love is unmet, and his efforts are discouraged until he feels depressed in hopeless despair.

The facts of mental illness must be honestly faced. One person out of every ten has some form of emotional illness needing psychiatric care. At any one time there are as many people in hospitals with mental illness as with all other diseases combined. Every year about 650,000 persons in the United States are admitted to hospitals for psychiatric treatment. Altogether in 1961 there were 1,450,000 persons who received such treatment in hospitals. In addition to these it is known that at least 50 percent of all the medical and surgical cases treated by private doctors and hospitals are complicated by emotional illness.[1]

[1] *Facts About Mental Illness* issued by the National Association for Mental Health, 10 Columbus Circle, New York 19, New York.

In some way all of these are lonely persons. But there are other lonely persons. It is well known that every third marriage ends in divorce. Not so familiar is the fact that every third young person quits high school before graduation, often becoming a displaced person who is not employable in a technological economy. Few realize that every eleventh person is over sixty-five years of age and that many of these people feel useless, lonely, and unwanted.

Loneliness is a prevailing condition in our society. Geographically, the density of population is greater as people live in crowded cities. Yet in moving to cities, we are uprooted from the communities where families once felt at home among friendly neighbors. Today we are likely to live among strangers who do not know or seem to care for each other in "the lonely crowd."

We have a strange fear of mental illness. Perhaps we are afraid because we know that we too are lonely persons. Unconsciously we shrink from the fear that loneliness may overcome us too. So we push the mentally ill away as if they were a plague to infect us with their intolerable fear. We send them to remote hospitals where they are locked up as outcasts from the society that drives them away. We seem to want to hide the person, look the other way and try to forget him, as if his suffering were too horrible to mention.

Loneliness was at the heart of Ellen West's mental illness.[2] She was described by her parents as a lively and headstrong child, yet she had days when everything seemed empty to her. At ten she moved with her family to Europe, where she went to

[2] Ludwig Binswanger, "The Case of Ellen West," in *Existence: A New Dimension in Psychiatry and Psychology*, ed. by Rollo May (New York: Basic Books, 1958), pp. 237-364.

a school for girls, was a good student, and wept if she was not the highest in her class. At seventeen she was writing poems in varying moods, her heart would beat with exultant joy, and then the sky would darken. She wrote of a confining tomb from which she would fly in a passionate desire for freedom. She changed from a deeply religious person to a complete atheist. There is a poem "Kiss me Dead," another "I Hate You," and a third one "Tired," set amid gray, damp, evening mists stretching out cold arms to her.

Her loneliness was hinted first when she felt that she could not stand to be alone or away from her parents. While on a visit to friends, she begged her parents to call her back to them. In a poem at twenty she yearned for a wild joy that would not dry up, "pining away bit by bit." "Oh, if He would come now," when every fiber of her is quivering.[3] In this year she became engaged to a romantic foreigner but gave him up at her father's wish. Her diary shows that she felt herself small and wholly forsaken in a world which she could not understand.

A new dread emerged when her girl friends teased her about getting fat. She had an enormous appetite, which she tried to deny, and took long walks alone to reduce her weight. She was constantly tormented, for the rest of her life, with the obsession of getting too fat; until, eating and vomiting and dieting and taking severe laxatives, she starved herself away from robust womanhood. In her diary she says that she had no home anywhere, even with her family. She felt herself absolutely worthless and useless. "I despise myself!" The only thing that still lured her was dying. "Death is the greatest happiness in life."[4]

She hated the luxury and good living that surrounded her, the

[3] *Ibid.*, p. 241.
[4] *Ibid.*, pp. 242-43.

cowardice, weakness, and hypocrisy. "I still feel the disgrace of my imprisonment. How musty is the smell of this cellar hole . . . . I want to go away, away—away from here." [5] At twenty-one she would have liked to forsake home and parents to live among the poorest of the poor. In searching for a cause to live for, she worked to install children's reading rooms in her town and tried other ventures to serve the poor.

At twenty-three she had a nervous breakdown after an unpleasant love affair with a riding teacher. A cloud of "depressive unrest" hung over her life. Then she found love and became engaged to a student, but her parents arranged a temporary separation. She went to a seaside resort in a severe depression, and at twenty-four she begged her parents to let her return. She did everything to get thin and arrived home in emaciated and tormented condition. The physician prescribed bed rest, and during six weeks in bed she wept constantly and gained weight. The engagement to the student was broken off. She went to a sanitarium and then to a school of gardening, but lost interest. The broken engagement remained an "open wound."

At twenty-eight she consented to marry her cousin, but she was not happy after the wedding. She continued to hate her body and to eat as little as possible, except in periods of uncontrolled eating. She had a miscarriage and was torn between the desire to have a child and the dread of getting fat. At thirty-one she felt a rapid decline in her strength. She gave up the two daily hikes with her husband, slept twelve hours a day, increased the laxatives and further reduced her diet. She looked old and haggard, and by the following year she weighed only ninety-two

[5] *Ibid.*, p. 245.

pounds. She began to go back to bed in the afternoon, feeling that "all real life had stopped."

Twice she undertook psychoanalysis but came to regard this as useless. "Often I am completely broken by the conflict which never comes to an end, and in despair I leave my analyst and go home with the certainty: he can give me discernment but not healing." [6] At thirty-three she walked aimlessly through the streets. She attempted suicide repeatedly by taking excess doses of barbiturates and throwing herself in front of passing cars. "My heart is full of despondency. . . . I attempt to satisfy two things while eating—hunger and love. Hunger gets satisfied—love does not! There remains the great unfilled hole." [7]

Another time she wrote: "I don't understand myself at all. It is terrible not to understand yourself. I confront myself as a strange person." [8] There were times when she seemed to recover her interest in life, as if something were stirring. "God grant that it may grow . . . . My heart throbs. Is love coming back into my life?" [9]

But then she would feel that she was withdrawing more and more from people. "I feel myself excluded from all real life. I am quite isolated. I sit in a glass ball. I see people through a glass wall, their voices come to me muffled. I have an unutterable longing to get to them. I scream but they do not hear me." [10]

Her diary reveals the pathos of her acute loneliness. Life had no further lure for her. "There is nothing, no matter where I look, which holds me . . . . Since I have buried myself in myself and can no longer find love, existence is only torture . . . . I am in

[6] *Ibid.*, p. 250.
[7] *Ibid.*, pp. 253-54.
[8] *Ibid.*
[9] *Ibid.*, pp. 255-56.
[10] *Ibid.*

prison, caught in a net from which I cannot free myself . . . . My heart is icebound, all around me is solitude and cold." [11]

She was sent to another sanitarium and she longed for death. She visited the locked wards and said, "I would want to smash in the solid panes immediately." [12] A medical consultation was held, and the danger of suicide recognized. But it was also agreed that placing her in a closed ward would not help her to recover. As the doctors could see no therapeutic usefulness in the commitment, they gave in to the patient's demand for discharge.

She returned home with her husband, enjoyed a walk with him, read her favorite poems, and wrote some letters. That night she took a lethal dose of poison, and the next morning she was dead.

2. *The Human Cry*

Human life begins with a cry. At the moment of birth there is travail and anguish in separating the child from the mother. They who had been one life, sustained by one bloodstream, are now two lonely persons. We welcome the first cry and rejoice in this waking of a new life to consciousness. Yet it is a cry of distress from a fearful stranger in a strange world. It is a cry of anger at being expelled from the womb, where every need was instantly and constantly met, into a cold and distant world where there are many unfulfilled needs and longings. It is a cry for warmth and nourishment, expressing a deep hunger for the answering response of tender loving care.

Is it too much to say the problem of loneliness begins at

[11] *Ibid.*, p. 258.
[12] *Ibid.*, p. 264.

birth? In our cult of individualism we may rejoice that now this child can be independent and have his own unique life to himself. He will have his own unique life, but can he really be independent? His deepest longings can only be fulfilled by interdependent relationships with other persons. He must be nourished from beyond himself or he will perish. He will cry again and again for someone to come to him and respond to his cry. If no one hears or cares enough to respond he will suffer acute rage and despair. Without the answering response of nourishing love he will waste away and want to die.

Suicide is a tragic loss. For the life full of potentialities, as yet unfulfilled, is cut off and cast aside. All of us are poorer to be robbed of a human life; the family and friends are plunged into grief and dismay. Yet to the person who takes the way of suicide, life has seemed hopeless and not worth the anguish and sorrow of living. The number and the agony of the persons who take this course is a matter of grave concern to our human community. Says Robert H. Felix, M.D., formerly Director of the National Institute of Mental Health, United States Public Health Service:

> Each year approximately 18,000 persons in the United States commit suicide. Each year one person in every ten thousand of our population carries out an irrevocable and awful decision to cease to live. Suicide is a major mental health problem in our country, as it is in most of the civilized nations of the world. It is an affliction that robs us of some of the most productive members of our community. It is a form of mental illness that is most disturbing to contemplate, a mental illness in which the anguish and terror of the victim lead him to prefer death to his suffering.[13]

[13] Preface to *The Cry for Help,* ed. by Norman L. Farberow and Edwin S. Shneidman (New York: McGraw Hill Book Company, 1961).

The number of attempted suicides is eight times that of committed suicides. This is the report of the Suicide Prevention Center in Los Angeles, whose workers respond, in cooperation with the police, hospitals, and community agencies, to every attempted suicide. They go to the person immediately to assist in his recovery and at the same time to learn what led up to the event. Every possible cause and clue is studied, including suicide notes, unheeded remarks, and evidence from interviews with the person, his family, and friends.

What they find is that suicide is a cry of anguish and hurt. The suicide attempt which falls short of death is a cry for help. Whatever form it may take, the cry is calling to someone to care. It is a cry for love and human response to save someone from despair and death.

In many cases suicide might have been prevented if someone had been alert and able to respond. A suicidal person is distressed and cries for help by planting clues, giving hints, and making attempts which are messages to someone to hear him and respond. Ellen West said, "I scream but no one hears me." Often these cries go unheeded, and if no one hears him or responds to his cry, the hopeless despair lures him to death.

To prevent suicide there is need for some person to care and have compassion on the one in distress. Someone who will hear the signals of distress, who will stand by to listen, to understand and respond with concern and empathy for the one who suffers this anguish. But many of us are too deaf to hear and too dumb to answer back. Busy as we are and preoccupied elsewhere, we go on ignoring and rejecting the person in need of someone to care.

We may be blocked by prejudice or by some of the many myths that surround suicide: people who talk about suicide never do it; suicide happens without warning; improvement after a suicide crisis means the risk is over; suicide occurs only when a person is depressed; all suicidal persons are insane; or suicide is immoral and can be controlled by legislation. These myths only discourage a suicidal person from seeking proper counsel and treatment.

What every person needs for health and wholeness are strong and sustaining interpersonal relationships. The wail of the newborn infant is the hunger-cry of everyone at every age for the answering response of love from someone who cares. The cry of suicide and mental illness represents the deep emotional distress of everyone who seeks to be "I and Thou." Every person is seeking a person. For persons sustain and re-create each other in the mutual response of community.

When there is no one to respond, life is empty and ultimately without meaning. The joy of wholeness is to be a person whose life is outgoing and inflowing through meaningful relationships. There is sorrow mingled with joy in every relationship, yet the potentiality of growth and fulfillment is worth the stress, if we uphold one another in responsive and faithful love. But where human ties weaken, we falter and fall away into lonely separation. As light and power come in a series of alternating currents, we are a living circuit that is no stronger than the weakest link of our relatedness.

There are two elements, as Carl Rogers says, in the loneliness of contemporary man.[14] One is an estrangement of man from himself, from his experiencing organism. To be loved by her parents, Ellen West had denied her own feelings and desires to love a man of her choice. This was a potentially fatal division,

[14] "The Loneliness of Contemporary Man." *Review of Existential Psychology and Psychiatry,* I (1961), 94-101.

when she took over her father's feelings as if they were her own. She evidently thought that she was in love but then found that, if she was to hold her father's love, she could not rely on her own experience to guide her. A person is very lonely when he cannot communicate with himself.

The other side of loneliness is the absence of a relationship in which one can communicate his experiencing to another. "When there is no relationship in which we are able to communicate both aspects of our divided self—both our conscious facade and our deeper level of experiencing—then we feel the loneliness of not being in real touch with any other human being." [15]

To reveal both sides of this loneliness, Rogers comments at length upon the case of Ellen West. In his previous writings he has emphasized the first separation within the person himself as an experiencing organism. I have emphasized the estrangement from and need for good relationships with other persons, but here he draws both sides of human loneliness into a perspective with which I heartily concur.

In breaking her engagements to please her father, Ellen had turned away from relationships with other persons who were significant to her. It was then she began eating too much in a vain effort to appease her hunger for love by food that did not satisfy this deeper need. Already distrusting herself, she was unable to withstand the teasing of her girl friends and came to fear she could never be loved if she were fat. This fear of a loveless life set up the endless conflict between the hunger for food and the hunger for love. Despair of love eventually separated her from parents, as well as potential lovers, her husband, and all

[15] *Ibid.*, p. 94.

other friends. She came to distrust others as she distrusted herself, until life became unbearable without either love or faith. Then how could she trust the analyst, who separated her from her husband, or the physicians, who knew she was suicidal yet set her free to kill herself as if they did not care for anything but to be rid of her.

She gave up being herself because no one accepted her as she was. When Rogers asks what went wrong with her treatment, he finds the greatest weakness was that "no one involved in her treatment seems to have related to her as a person; a person worthy of respect, a person capable of autonomous choice, a person whose inner experiencing is a precious resource to be drawn upon and trusted. Rather, she seems to have been dealt with as an object." [16]

He then considers how he could have proceeded if she had come to him at twenty-four when she had sought medical help. He would have accepted her as she was, actually and potentially, and been willing for her to be both. As her feelings were heard and understood, he believes that she would have been able to express her deeper conflicts and see that she could both love and resent her father; that her desires to be dependent and independent, her hunger to eat and her fear of being fat and ugly could all be accepted. Instead of struggling against her nature, she could have accepted and lived with her feelings as a person who is open to accept her own experiences.

In a relationship where all of herself was accepted, she could feel "safe to communicate herself more completely. She would discover that she did not need to be lonely and isolated—that another could understand and share the meaning of her ex-

[16] *Ibid.*, p. 98.

perience, . . . that it is . . . far more satisfying to be one's real self in relating to others." [17]

We need not apologize for our confidence in the power of relationship. In an earlier chapter I confessed my faith in a psychology and theology of relationship. We may see how psyche and theos are interrelated when we note that Ellen changed from a deeply religious person into an atheist, at the very time she became estranged from the open communication of interdependent human relations. The I-Thou relation is everywhere fulfilling, and its denial is everywhere defeating and dehumanizing.

The best hope for Ellen's recovery and personal fulfillment would have been in a creative person-to-person relationship. There are lessons to learn from her life and death. The first of these lessons is stated by Rogers.

> In every respect in which we make an object of the person—whether by diagnosing him, analyzing him, or perceiving him impersonally in a case history—we stand in the way of our therapeutic goal. To make an object of a person has been helpful in treating physical ills. It has not been successful in treating psychological ills. We are deeply helpful only when we relate as persons, when we risk ourselves as persons in the relationship, when we experience the other as a person in his own right. Only then is there a meeting of a depth which dissolves the pain of aloneness in both client and therapist.[18]

What are the prospects of recovery from mental illness? They are as good as those is any other illness. With good care, at least seven out of ten patients can leave a mental hospital with-

[17] *Ibid.*, p. 100.
[18] *Ibid.*, p. 101.

in an average time of four months or less. The chances of recovery from schizophrenia have leaped from 20 percent to 70 percent. Rates of readmission can be reduced from 35 percent of the patients discharged to 10 percent with good rehabilitation service and aftercare.[19]

But how good is the care we give mental patients? Only ten percent of our general hospitals admit psychiatric patients. Of the 277 state mental hospitals only 20 percent are giving truly therapeutic care. Many do not have the budgets or treatment staff to become a therapeutic community. In the whole of our country there were, in 1961, only 1,400 outpatient mental health clinics. Many of these are part-time, and most of them have long waiting lists.

If you or I should become mentally ill, as one out of ten of us will, what kind of care do we have a right to expect? We would hope for the best of care, consonant with the medical and health services for any other illness. We, like everyone else, would be entitled to the best care which all professions working together can provide in the most democratic and generous of nations. We would want others to care for us as faithfully and compassionately as we care for them.

3. *Puzzling Questions*

Who is responsible for mental illness and health? Was Ellen West responsible for her mental illness? Or her parents, her school friends, her lovers, her husband, the physicians, or God?

[19] This information is from a national survey by the Joint Commission of Mental Illness and Health authorized by Congress in 1955. See *Action for Mental Health* (New York: Basic Books, 1961).

And was she responsible to make herself well? Or the other persons in her life? Or God?

These are puzzling questions to wrestle with. It seems unfair to blame a person for making himself ill; it is like striking a man when he is down. And yet a person may often hold himself accountable and ask, What have I done to bring this upon me? It may be that feelings of guilt and self-rejection enter into the distress of the illness.[20] It may be that the stress of interpersonal relations will affect us for good or ill. Can it be that we make each other sick or well? Are we interdependent members one of another in a social organism where we sustain or infect each other with contagious influences?

A theology of relationship will be asking these questions too. The disciples were asking Jesus about the blind man there before them: "Rabbi, who sinned, this man or his parents?" (John 9:2). Many blame the person who is ill or in distress, the alcoholic, the neurotic, the criminal, the suicidal person. There are others who incline to blame the parents who brought him into the world and who brought him up in the formative years. Somehow we tend to feel better when we project the responsibility on someone else.

But Jesus would have none of this casting blame like stones at a person in trouble. It was neither this man nor his parents who sinned and brought this affliction upon him. This is not the occasion to blame anyone; to do so is misleading. There is a mystery about illness and health that with all our knowledge and favorite theories we cannot penetrate. It is just as misleading to blame God or fate or karma. To blame anyone is only to add insult to injury and compound the hurt by attacking those who

[20] See O. Hobart Mowrer, *The Crisis in Psychiatry and Religion* (New York: D. Van Nostrand, 1961).

suffer. Blaming another is pointing the finger over there to protect ourselves that we may escape notice.

Blame leads us away from our responsibility. "Am I my brother's keeper? Let him suffer and die if he will, but keep far away from me; I am not the one to suffer." So we reject the one who suffers and deny his pain as not ours. But it is inhuman not to care what others suffer. It denies the whole meaning of community, that we belong to each other, that we are brothers who care for one another in every condition. The one who suffers is the one who belongs to us, and we will suffer with him. We care for him because we are deeply related to each other in our common life as a caring community. If he is our man, we do not turn away from him in fearful disgust. We come to him in faithful love to accept him as he is, to suffer with him, to help, and to heal.

Whoever is ill or afflicted becomes my responsibility. He offers me the greatest opportunity that ever comes to one, to rise above petty, selfish smallness and be a great human person who cares for other persons. It was in this light that Jesus saw the blind beggar. He did not turn the other way and pass by. He accepted him with loving compassion, though a stranger, and stretched out his hand to help him. He saw the man related to God as well as to the human community. His affliction did not mean that God had forsaken him, but rather that God cared the more for him. God suffered with him, and calls us to suffer with others like him in one unbroken life of love. The person who suffers any need is an opportunity for God as well as man to hear the cry and respond to him with loving care. We may act with God to help him, that the healing work of God may be manifest in him (John 9:3). So Jesus worked and suffered with God for fellowman.

If we are human we know how it feels to be hurt. When I skin my knee or shin, I know what it is to be distressed and angry. But there is a deeper hurt. The skin is surface pain, soon to heal over and be forgotten as a temporary discomfort. But to be misunderstood or put down as unworthy, to be closed out from love and unforgiven, is a deeper hurt. It becomes anxiety, anguish, and despair.

This is person-hurt far deeper than skin-hurt: to be alone and separate with none to care, to be in a mental hospital or prison and no one to call on me, to be a failure and no one to give me another chance to make a new start. This is breaking the heart, shattering the very center of my life, until I feel as good as dead, hopeless, and estranged from life where other persons live.

Only a person can heal person-hurt. There is no medicine but love, though we try everything else. We need someone with compassion enough to care, who will not give us up as useless and unreclaimable but will uphold us in faithful love. If we have been hurt we need a caring community. We have, every one of us, been hurt. We know what it means to smart with shame and suffer in despair. We can share the hurt of others if we are willing. But often we are not willing. We prefer our ease and comfort, shielding ourselves from the pain that others suffer.

From what do persons suffer most? The most hurt is in human relations, between husband and wife, parent and child, brother and sister in the family. The larger society is, in fact, the extension of our human family. Seeking again and again to be whole, we project and continue the stress and hunger of family living into all our relationships wherever we meet.

How do we respond to persons who hurt? We know the way of blame and rejection, so familiar as to be chronic, and so futile as to frustrate persons in every new anger and despair.

Parents and teachers label children as bad, when they act out their feelings. Our society locks up the criminal, where he hates the more and learns to be the more determined offender. It has been customary to blame the mental patient for his strange behavior and put him out of sight and mind in closed wards where he suffers rejection, excluded from family and society.

There is another way, the way of accepting, understanding, and empathy. If you are physically sick, you invite help and usually cooperate as a good patient. If you are mentally ill, you may be hostile or withdrawn in bizarre behavior that repels the one who seeks to help you. We must really want to accept the one who is hurt, or it will be easier to avoid him and leave him to his lonely misery. If we really want to accept him, we must go out of our way to find him and be with him.

This is what Albert Schweitzer did in leaving his attractive career as musician and theologian to go to Lambaréné and bring a ministry of healing to the sick of equatorial Africa. He speaks of our sense of responsibility to those who suffer as that which we have no ethical right to ignore. He rests his case upon two basic principles that are so universal they touch everyone and bring all life into one community. The first of these is the principle of reverence for life. The wonder and potentiality of life call forth our deepest reverence. The second is the fellowship of pain. All who suffer pain are drawn together in one indivisible life of mutual caring. Because we share the hurt of pain, we are called to respond to others in their pain. Each one who knows pain is bound to share and bear the pain of another, to carry the burden with him and to let him know he is not alone, for someone knows what he suffers.

Our responsibility to those who suffer transcends all boundaries of race, nation, and religion, wherever we accept our full membership in the community of man. This we see in the parable of the good Samaritan, where it was the foreigner who was neighbor enough to show mercy to the wounded man by the Jericho Road. The parable does not pursue the criminals to punish them but holds the focus steadily upon the question, Who will help the wounded man? Yet our first response to a highway accident or a television mystery story is, Who is the guilty one to punish?

This desire to blame, as we have seen, is misleading in the deepest sense. Projecting blame on others leads away from me and denies my own responsibility, which is the real issue. The profoundest meaning of community is that we belong to one another in the mutual relatedness of our humanity. You and I are responsible to each other, wherever and whoever we are. To be responsible is to be able to respond. It is the spiritual dimension that distinguishes man from animal. The distinctive character of the human spirit is responsibility.[21]

Out of this responsibility of the human spirit hospitals are built and medical centers are open to those who suffer in mind and body. Because they are human in the finest sense, people offer themselves to be physicians and psychiatrists, nurses and medical technicians, psychologists, and social workers. In this spirit of responsibility pastors and theological students come to hospitals and prisons to meet face-to-face those who suffer, and learn with other helping professions in clinical pastoral training how to respond to those who are hurt.

The founder of this clinical pastoral education was Anton T. Boisen[22] in 1925. A minister who himself suffered mental illness, he became the pioneer full-time chaplain to mental

[21] See Frankl, *The Doctor and the Soul.*
[22] *Out of the Depths* (New York: Harper & Brothers, 1960).

patients. With Richard C. Cabot,[23] he invited theological students to a clinical internship in the hospital where they could learn to accept, understand, and minister to those who suffer the crises of illness.

4. *Faithful Love*

There are two moods in human life that come forth in our responses to other persons. There is the mood of rugged independence to stand alone against others, to keep up a bold front, repress our emotions, and hide our problems. This is the frontier virtue of self-reliance, to press on alone whatever the dangers and hardships may be. The aim is to lead with strength, to struggle against competitors, to deny every need, and fight the harder to prove one is able. "God helps those who help themselves" is the motto of this way of life.

The other is the response of humility to confess need and seek help. In this mood we welcome the privilege of cooperation in a community of mutual respect and concern. When we are able to trust each other we can lay aside our defenses and be open to speak from the heart our true feelings. We can listen more deeply to what the other person is trying to communicate. In this mood of sharing we can lay open the problem and reveal our concern to another person. "Two heads are better than one" is the motto of this way of life. Talking it out with another person is a new way of looking at life in larger perspective, to see more clearly and decide more wisely.

A nationwide study has been made of these two moods by the

[23] *Adventures on the Borderlands of Ethics* (New York: Harper & Brothers, 1926)

Joint Commission of Mental Illness and Health.[24] Self-help is characteristic of older men, living in rural areas, with less education. The readiness to talk about one's problems and seek professional help is more characteristic of younger persons who have at least a high school education and live in urban areas. They seem to reflect the mood of modern life that we are members of an open community where we may trust other persons and be free to talk with them of our personal lives. Acute distress is not the primary index, but rather a willingness to be open and to talk in a trusting mood with others in open and secure relationships.

What this seems to reveal is that no person can be complete in himself if he holds himself apart in "splendid isolation." Mental health is not for one alone. The lonely person cannot be whole or healthy. We live in and from the deeper oneness of life together. The self-contained person is fragmentary and undernourished in the larger resources of health.

Mental health is the progressive achievement by a growing person of mature selfhood and enriching relationships with other persons. This is the inalienable right of every person whatever his age, place, or condition. Each person has sensitive capacities to awaken and potential strengths to develop, if he is to fulfill his true nature. This cannot be done alone but is achieved in sound relationships with other persons who respect and encourage one another.

We have not done as well as we know how to do for the mentally ill. Humane healing care has not been adequately provided. Instead, the ill have been disowned as too difficult to

[24] This study is reported by Gerald Gurin, *et al.*, *Americans View Their Mental Health.*

live with. Yet there is no way to find mental health in the remote confines of the isolation ward.

Mental health is for all, together in a caring community. Only as we care for each other do we become more healthy and whole. Mental health is people caring for people. Mental health is the growing fruit of a community where persons accept and love and trust each other. Healthy persons make a good community, and a good community makes healthy persons.

What is the role of the church in mental health? Mental health as here defined is a primary concern of the Christian church.[25] In the continuing work of its historic mission the church has sought the true fulfillment of growing persons in all the relationships of life. The biblical writings, from the first to the last page, express interest in the salvation of the whole person. A theology of salvation through relationship is the motive of the church's concern for mental health in the largest sense. The ultimate cause of human eccentricity is that man is out of his true center in God. The surest path to wholeness is that which brings man to his place within the circle of redemptive love, divine and human. In its ministry to suffering, distraught persons the church seeks to become a channel of the healing work of God.

The church is to be a meeting of people. It is a going forth from one's hiding place to meet other persons openly, to know them face-to-face, and to accept them as they are. When we are hurt we may run away, pull back, and withdraw from exposure. It is tragic to see older persons retire into lonely isolation, take cover, hide in a distant retreat, and keep apart. It is sad to see a young person close himself in sullen resentment of and resistance

[25] For a good treatment of this see Howard Clinebell, *Mental Health Through Christian Community* (Nashville: Abingdon Press, 1965).

to his family. It is foreboding to see a child who is quiet and withdrawn, not free to participate openly and easily in his class at school or his group on the playground. The church calls us forth from holding back, to come toward each other, to be open to God and others, to confess our mistakes rather than hide sin and failure, and go forward as one people.

The church is to be a fellowship of faithful love. We may see the church as a building on the corner, set apart and closed except for Sunday. But this is a very limited view of the church. Actually the church is *the people* who come in and then go forth to the world in faithful love. The church is persons who care for persons enough to hold together faithfully, to love and never stop loving whatever one does or whoever one is, to be every one a servant to the other, to minister each to all and all to each. Every member is to be a minister ready to accept and to serve another, to stand by the one who is hurt and care for him in love. C. W. Brister speaks of the pastoral action of the church.

> The Christian *koinonia*, by its very nature, implies a shared ministry by the pastor and his people; . . . each layman is to *be* the church where he lives and works. . . . The interrelatedness of ministry . . . is to be understood in corporate rather than individualistic terms. . . . All Christians are custodians of the answers to human woe. . . . I believe that persons can find dignity and meaning in concrete acts of love. . . . It takes courage to care, as well as to share one's suffering with another. . . . In pastoral care, courage implies being secure enough to make oneself available to a suffering person in a loving relationship.[26]

The church is to join in healing the hurts of life: first in person-to-person care, where I go to you and you come to me in

[26] *Pastoral Care in the Church* (New York: Harper & Row, 1964), pp. 84, 90, 94, 100, 104, 105.

my need, to keep in touch, responding and upholding our common life together; then in strengthening the larger community in the total work of healing, planning how to be a true community of people who intentionally live together, promoting and developing the community resources such as hospitals, social agencies, mental health clinics, and pastoral counseling centers so urgently needed. Persons will need to encourage each other to serve on committees, as aides and volunteers, in community-wide appeals and as sponsors to sustain these facilities. The aim must be to change the entire approach toward mental illness, to replace the closed ward of isolating rejection with open mental health centers for outpatient day care. The emotionally disturbed must be welcomed back into the family and a loving effort made to accept one another. This is to give up prejudice and punitive blame for a new spirit of empathy and acceptance.

As we dare to get close to those who are deeply troubled, or let them get close to us, we hear over and over again something of the dreadful story involved in the inability to love. We learn what it means to be shut up in the prison of the self so that life ends up in the farce of settling for intimacy without relationship, and the ultimate blasphemy of suffering relationships that have no intimacy. It is in just these areas that we need desperately to learn from those who have so violently protested against these indecencies. It is just here that the sanity of the insane has so much to offer by way of illuminating the insanity of the sane! [27]

The role of the church is to infuse the whole human community with spiritual resources of hope, faith, and love. We do not have enough hope or faith or love. So, we falter in fear and

[27] Ernest E. Bruder, *Ministering to Deeply Troubled People* (Englewood Cliffs, N.J.: Prentice-Hall, 1963), pp. 23-24.

anxiety, or we turn back in lonely despair or fall apart in conflict and competition where we most need reconciliation and love. The church can be a loving fellowship to infuse the human community, if each one within it will care for the hurt of another and respond in a spirit of mutual concern. The church is not to be a rival to other agencies and services. There should be no warring of sects but rather interfaith and interdiscipline teamwork by all groups living and working together. If the church is a living community of faithful love, it will bring new life to the entire community of man.

6
The Responsibility of the Counselor

1. To Be Responsible

We can agree that the counselor must be responsible. Persons turn to him for help with urgent problems of greatest concern to them in the crises and perplexities of human life. They come with their fragile hopes and their fears that all may be lost unless they find a better way.

When the counselor is a pastor his responsibility is even greater. We have noted the nationwide survey showing that persons with emotional problems go to the pastor more than to other professionals. When asked why they come to the pastor they said, Because we know him and trust him.[1] This is a crisis for the pastor. He must ask himself, "Am I competent to fulfill these expectations?"

The pastor intends to be responsible. He has met the require-

[1] Gurin *et al.*, *Americans View Their Mental Health*, p. 307.

ments of ordination as a minister of the church. He has been to school and taken the required courses. He has been examined, approved, and authorized to minister to the spiritual needs of the people. He has taken vows to be a faithful servant of all, to instruct and guide the people in the true way of life, to care for those in distress, and to strengthen the faltering.

The pastoral counselor has added responsibilities in the face-to-face encounter of counseling. He is called upon to give himself in close relation to the deep and complex emotional needs of those who come to him. How far shall he go? Where does he draw the line and set the limits? Does he bear unlimited responsibility for every person who asks or presents a need? What are his specific responsibilities? Where do they begin and end? Or are they endless, making an almost infinite demand upon his resources?

Questions of responsibility are more than abstract academic issues. They are personal and social questions of great moment in crucial and urgent human situations. They break in upon us with terrific and compelling force, shaking the foundations, cracking our well-established defenses, pressing upon us until there is no escape.

What is the responsibility toward the man who asked for pastoral counseling after the doctors had been unable to help him with a dangerous condition of ulcerative colitis? Or the highly trained medical specialist who was unable to establish his practice due to conflict with his wife? What of the nurse who committed suicide after two sessions at a pastoral counseling center? Or the woman who could not bear the grief of her daughter's death, and the accusation of a friend who said, "Your faith might have saved her?"

A pastor on the way to his evening counseling slowed down

for an intersection, when suddenly out of the dark a man stepped in front of the car. There was no time to swerve before the impact. First aid was given with oxygen, and he was taken to the hospital by ambulance for emergency treatment, but he died an hour later. At the next case conference the pastoral counselor told how for twelve years he had been ministering to this man in and out of prisons and hospitals. "After doing all this to save him, I am now the cause of his death," he lamented.

"But the accident was unavoidable," the other counselors said. "There was nothing you could do. The police and the judge agree you were not negligent or irresponsible in any way."

"Yet I do feel responsible," the pastor said, "and this is a burden I cannot cast off. What more can I do? I have met the police, the judge, and the registry officer; I have ministered to the family, confessed to God, and now to you, my brother ministers. I will still minister to others as God may permit, but will they trust me now?"

After weighing the matter, the pastors concluded, "It is our task to ease the anguish and not to punish ourselves unduly with accusing guilt. We must accept the burden and carry it as those who know grief and can bear sorrow. In the moments of deepest distress at the cruel necessities of human life, we must somehow be reconciled to live through these times, at peace with God and man."

"You were going for us," they said, "to represent our council of churches as a ministering community. We must be willing to take the risks of serving and suffering, for the sake of all who are linked with us in our human destiny."

It is events like this that press upon a counselor, causing him to ask more seriously than ever before, "Am I a responsible person in my life and work? Is this a responsible pastoral counseling center? Am I caring enough and bearing enough? Do I minister wisely and well to others, in the stress and mutual responsibility of those who seek to become one body, a true community of God and man?"

How does the counselor fulfill his responsibility? What does it mean for the counselor to be responsible?

1. To be a responsible counselor is to respond with my whole being to the person before me at this moment. He may be a stranger but he has full claim upon me. For this hour and this person I am called to give my best. There are times when it is not convenient. Once when Martin Buber was in prayer and meditation, a student came to see him but was turned away with instructions to return at a later time. The student did not return, however; he committed suicide. Then Buber asked, "Does God turn us away from his creatures?"

> That is sublimely to misunderstand God. Creation is not a hurdle on the road to God, it is the road itself. We are created along with one another and directed to a life with one another. Creatures are placed in my way so that I, their fellow-creature, by means of them and with them find the way to God.[2]

It is true we have many responsibilities which often seem to be in conflict. In the midst of these multiple demands upon our time and attention, it is not easy to sort them out or resolve the conflicts. One basic rule, I find, is to be fully present to the person before me. I try to concentrate with utmost intensity as a unified person, and not yield to distraction. For this reason it is well to have no telephone in the counseling room. An effort

[2] Martin Buber, *Between Man and Man*, tr. by R. G. Smith (New York: The Macmillan Company, 1947), p. 52. Used by permission of The Macmillan Company and Routledge and Kegan Paul.

should be made to avoid covert glances to the agenda beyond this hour, to be free of darting mind-wandering.

A responsible person is one who is able to respond in this hour with the integrated unity of all his resources flowing into the course of the life before him. Viktor Frankl spells responsibility as two words, response-ability, to focus upon our ability to respond. Martin Buber spells out the meaning this way:

> Genuine responsibility exists only where there is real responding. Respond to what? To what happens to one, to what is seen and heard and felt. Each concrete hour allotted to the person, with its content drawn from the world and from destiny, is speech for the man who is attentive. . . . It will, then, be expected of the attentive man that he faces creation as it happens. It happens as speech, not as speech rushing out over his head but as speech directed precisely at him.
>
> Responsibility presupposes one who addresses me primarily, that is, from a realm independent of myself, and to whom I am answerable. He addresses me about something that he has entrusted to me and that I am bound to take care of loyally.
>
> The human person belongs . . . to the community in which he is born or which he has happened to get into. . . . He must put his arms around the vexatious world, whose true name is creation, only then do his fingers reach the realm of lightning and grace. . . . He must face the hour which approaches him, the biographical and historical hour, just as it is. . . . You must hear the claim, however unharmoniously it strikes the ear—and let no one interfere; give the answer from the depths, where a breath of what has been breathed in still hovers—and let no one prompt you.
>
> God tenders me the situation to which I have to answer; but I

balance as one who understands the hidden implications and interrelationships in true perspective.

Counseling is rigorous work. It is labor of the hardest kind to keep a steady focus on the person in spite of distractions and complexities; listening deeply to understand, upholding his distress in a relaxed and trusting relationship, struggling with his ambivalences in response to other persons, searching for alternative ways through the difficulty with growing insight and ability to decide. It is useless to give advice and attempt to solve his problem for him with a ready answer that is only a verbal solution in order to conclude the matter and hasten on to the next problem. Counseling goes deeper, broader, higher, and farther than external advice. The intellectual answer is easy, but it is superficial and oversimplifying. It does not engage the whole person with all his relationships, or stand by him in the ongoing earch for his unique destiny among his fellows.

The true goal of counseling is growth in all dimensions of fe. No minor adjustment or reduction of symptoms will do, ateful as we are for every step forward no matter how small. hat we seek is a radical cure to become mature and whole, er and stronger, more free and responsible, more creative and urceful to meet future problems as they arise. In religious s, we want salvation of the whole person in all his relation- s, to God as the ultimate Thou, and to every human thou in ncounters of his daily living. There must be uncovering for erson to know himself more deeply; yet it must not be a t unmasking or clever exposure of his secret, but rather a and patient searching faithfully together. There will be ities, vague fears, false expectations, and uncertainties what to do or how to go forward together. These will be verbalized and worked through until we can see our

have not to expect that he should tender me anything of my answer. . . . I answer for my hour.[3]

Not until this hour do I know its meaning. For it is only now that I can experience this hour. My response to the person before me in this hour comes out of this hour as we experience it together. Yet my response must always be in reference to the larger perspective of my relation to God, and to the community of all the persons around me with whom I stand in the ultimate demands of our human venture.

2. A responsible counselor will meet the person with profound reverence. I must withhold hasty or partial judgments, seeing the person with clear eye, free of personal bias or the squint of shortsighted vision. I must follow his lead, searching with him, going at his pace in self-effacing patience to understand more deeply. I must stand in his place to see what life means to him, to know what he is feeling and suffering, to care with genuine compassion, and bear with him the full stress of his existential situation.

To be responsible I must hold his life story in complete confidence as privileged communication to cherish. I must honor the seal of the confessional, protecting him in every unguarded moment from a careless word or damaging rumor. There will need to be consultation with professional colleagues to serve him best, yet always with his consent, as we search together and work together for larger understanding and more open communication.

In every consideration of the person we must let him stand in

[3] *Ibid.*, pp. 16, 45, 65-66, 68-69. These sentences are somewhat rearranged to carry the essential thought forward.

the best and truest light. It is not for me to be a detective to trap him into a forced confession against his will, or to uncover secrets he is not yet ready to reveal. I am to be for him as his counselor, without prejudice or partiality, seeking to understand the whole situation in balanced perspective. Am I willing to let him be the person he is, at the same time expecting and engaging him to be a growing person? Do I itch impatiently to change him or manipulate him toward a goal I have chosen for him. Or can I let him be what he is, accept and respect him as he seeks to be the person he wants to become?

3. As his counselor am I able to trust him whatever he may do? He may not trust me or my church or my God, yet it is not for me, through counseling, to compel him to believe. He has the right to follow his own conscientious conviction as an open person who can be honest with himself and free to declare his position.

He may turn against me, defy what I would have him do and resist my desire to help him. He may fail again and again to reach his goals or move in the direction he seeks to go. Am I responsible enough to trust him in spite of everything, to let my trust be contagious and pervasive and unwavering under all conditions, in the face of whatever disappointments we have to meet? This is not to be blind to his faults or to deny his fearful or angry feelings which may be acted out impulsively; it is to trust the hidden potential for growth in him even when all is known.

Can I be an open person as the counselor; not covering up my true feelings under a professional manner, but dealing freely and honestly with myself and with him? Can I accept his anxiety without becoming fearful, and his hostility without retaliation or estrangement? Will there be inner strength to bear the load of

his distress without weakness or despair? Basic trust is the bridge of a sound relationship. It is prerequisite to every other good we seek in counseling. It is not blind or naïve belief, for this is as careless and deceptive as living a lie, but honest truth-seekin together, giving a trusting spirit to this person, as he is and m potentially become. I must believe in him as a responsi spirit, though deeply embroiled in conflict; who, within limits, is free to choose who he will be. I must see him as who is able to be a true person in the midst of his difficulti to bear tragic suffering with inherent dignity.

4. A responsible counselor will engage the person dialogue for the sake of growth. It is not enough to be listener who is inert, evasive, or noncommittal, giv nothing but vague signals like the "educated grunt." icant that Carl Rogers discarded "nondirective" co "client-centered" therapy, to participate in a more proach. We have seen the need for a responsive enter more fully into the searching engagement w What we seek is not a monologue by either th counselor, but a real dialogue of two-way commu

True counseling is nothing less than exis where each person is to give himself to the with the dilemmas and counterforces of hum hold an "interview" if not to exchange active and responsible persons? What do w "session" to be? The word comes from th sitting of a court. This is not just sitting dozing in the sun. It means to sit in t counselor, to hear the person as he sta complex ramifications of it, and t

way more clearly to define goals, clarify the relationship, and change the focus to more crucial and central issues.

5. The counselor is responsible for the limits of the counseling relationship. He cannot let the anxious person control the relation to the extent of the young woman who felt she must go around the world with her counselor to continue the relationship. Who is to decide in matters that affect the many complex relationships of these lives? There are some issues the person must decide for himself, if they are his responsibility. Yet there are other questions the counselor must decide when they are his responsibility. The counselor in these questions has to draw a firm line and hold it without swerving. Limits of time serve a dynamic urgency in growth, as do limits of favors and affection. Limits of responsibility are essential to a sound relationship. If the limits are not defined we are overwhelmed and confused, angry and despairing of the unmanageable situation. If the seeking person is to grow, the counselor must give authority without abdicating his own. He must sustain and confront the quest to become a more responsible person.

Freud has shown the value of "transference" in the counseling relationship. He shows how the past must be intensely relived in the present relationship, so that the person may be free of the past and enabled to live in the present, according to the reality principle. Another transference will be urgently needed in our counseling: the transfer of the present learning into the future in order to move from this relationship outward to other persons with the dialogue of true encounter.

A responsible counselor will be working steadily to transfer his authority to the growing person, who must become responsible for his own decisions in the crucial areas of his life. At the same time, the counselor trusts him to transfer what is learned in this counseling relationship to every other relationship into which he will be going. The counselor does not aim to be the star player. He is the coach who invests his life in the growth of other persons who are to carry the ball and make the touchdowns. The responsible counselor is one who spends himself fully, not for his own gain or advantage, but that others may grow. If he would save others he cannot care about saving himself. This we learn from the Man on the cross.

2. *Learning and Teaching*

The goal of counseling is growth. A person may grow physically with proper nourishment and exercise. Yet more is needed than chemicals and the stretching of muscles. It has been demonstrated that infants will waste away and die without tender loving care.[4] Nourishing of the spirit and exercise of the mind are essential to physical growth. The growth we seek in counseling is the total growth of the whole person.

Learning is the heart of all human growth. What the baby inherits is potentiality; for nothing is complete at birth. Each new individual is launched upon a lifelong course of becoming a person. His life story will be unique because he meets every event in his own way, by learning for himself how he will respond. In all this learning he is involved with other persons in the intricate design of human relations. Parents and others are usually there to call him forth from inertia, to waken his responses, to invite his first steps and words, to show him how to act and engage him in the many adventures of learning. Yet he

[4] Margaretha Ribble, *The Rights of Infants* (New York: Columbia University Press, 1943).

often resists learning, angry at being disturbed or corrected, weary of demands upon his solitude, and stubbornly insisting on his way against the guiding pressure of family culture and social conformity.

By the time a person comes to a counselor he is deeply entangled in the dilemmas of his complex relationships with other persons, who push and pull him in contrary ways. In the maze of these conflicting forces within and around him, he seeks a clearer way to cut through the Gordian knot of this tangle. He has been hurt enough to be angry and defiant, he is anxious and cautious not to expose himself to more hurt. From this distress comes a need to understand what is going on, to see himself and the other persons more truly, to sort out his feelings, and know what he wants to do with his life. From such a situation he comes to a counselor with a new readiness to learn.

It is clear that psychotherapy is a form of learning. A person comes to learn about himself in the midst of his own unique life situation. He may be fed up with other forms of learning, at school or home or work, where he is told what to do and believe. Yet he seeks a new kind of learning that will be relevant for him, where he chooses the subjects, assigns the tasks, searches for the answers, and enters a dialogue on his own terms to wrestle with the meaning and responsible choices of his acute existence. In this learning process he will grow, if he can invest his full powers, with all the intensity of his being, in the dynamic interchange of face-to-face encounter.

The counselor knows that he can be no teacher in the traditional style of one who lectures, gives out library work, grades papers, and has the last word. Yet he must be teaching if the learning is to be effective—a new kind of teaching in response to a new and deeply personal learning. Like a tutor, his counseling is oriented to one person who offers himself for private instruction, though his instruction is not confined to abstract ideas but extends to issues of the utmost concern to the person in his own context of life. Like a research team they seek to discover the true facts, and search insistently for the meaning of the whole field of interacting forces and meanings.

The person defines the problem and sets the course of learning desired. The counselor is the consultant who listens with open mind, considers the goals and ways of proceeding to them, examines alternatives, draws upon a fund of expert knowledge, and devotes himself fully to the needs of the person.

The counselor cannot rest, however, upon his previous knowledge, no matter how extensive or well indexed or available for ready use. The problem goes far beyond "Information Please," because it is in reality an ongoing quest for new life in which to outgrow the old life. We may call this existential learning for it involves all of life and takes place only in the midst of life that is lived at this moment. For each quest of ongoing discovery, the answer does not exist before its hour, and then it arises out of the revealings, the projectings, and emergings of this hour. Such a wrestling with and for a human destiny is no exchange of information or social pleasantries, no external advice, no easy platitudes, no vapid reassurance that all will be well if you relax and ventilate the pent-up feelings. The struggle for growth is no child's play of fantasy (though we need to recover the child within us), but the full engagement of the whole life in vigorous analysis and vital fulfillment.

It is a tragic mistake for the counselor to assume that learning is only for the other person. Unless the counselor learns as much as the counselee, unless both engage in a discipline of mutual learning where each is willing to submit himself to the arduous requirements of faithful learning, the whole endeavor will fail. We can see in any form of education that teaching does not automatically provide learning, nor do students learn unless the teacher is learning along with them. So the counselor must learn of the person if the person is to learn of the counselor. Time may be wasted in counseling as well as in the classroom unless both parties are ready and able to learn from the encounter. Those who teach can learn much from the approach of the counselor to learning.

The counselor awakens initiative in the person who seeks to grow. He accepts him as he is and starts where the person wants to begin. He invites him to present himself with his problem, to *be* the question he is asking, to formulate out of his own life experience the issues that state his concern. The counselor listens intently and patiently while the person struggles to express his feelings and define his goals. He listens without interrupting to give quick answers or ready conclusions. He does not hasten to change the subject, but dwells at length upon the detailed events the person is living through as he reveals and elaborates them to the counselor. As they come to the heart of the matter, both will enter into living dialogue in the mutual address and response of two-way communication. If the dialogue is one-sided or blocked at any point, they will need to focus upon the barriers and their reactions to each other, to see the meaning of their mode of relating to each other. Goals will be redefined, progress will be reviewed, issues restated, growing insights clarified, alternatives weighed, and action foreseen in reference to the responsible decisions to be made as they move forward in the counseling. Eventually, they will consider when to terminate the counseling. They must then consider what can be learned from it in final perspective, whether to refer to other counselors and resources, how to extend this learning to other relationships, and what to project into the future as new steps toward new goals.

For this kind of learning and teaching the counselor will need a special preparation. He must submit himself ardently and faithfully to the lessons of his own discipline, if he is to enter fully into the learning process and all of the urgencies of another life. To meet this test he must prepare himself by confrontation through long hours of searching dialogue with many persons.

When is the best time to prepare for the work of counseling? Time, in reality, is not cut up into the chunks or blocks we denote in making up a daily schedule. Living time is endless, as continuous as the ongoing stream of experience and events shaping our growing lives. It is well to prepare as early as possible in thorough academic and clinical training integrated around personal identity so that the pastoral counselor can know who he is, and what his responsibility is in this vocation. Yet his time of learning can never end; rather it must continue every day and hour to be up-to-date and contemporary.

What is the best way to prepare for pastoral counseling? The American Association of Pastoral Counselors has, through its working committees and annual meetings, been defining standards for membership in the association. College and theological education are recognized as a minimum, with relevant graduate study leading to a master's or doctor's degree desirable. Three years of parish experience in a recognized denomination or faith group is required. There must be evidence of a continuing, responsible relationship to the religious community. Three to six months in an accredited center for clinical pastoral training will be required, and 125 to 400 hours of interdisciplinary supervision of one's pastoral counseling, dealing with the religious and psychological dimensions of human problems. Personal psychotherapy is strongly recommended to show the counselor his intrapsychic life and protect the counselee from those problems. He will also need to understand the counseling process, and have ability to develop a counseling relationship.

The following statement of standards was presented at the annual meeting of the American Association of Pastoral Counselors in Chicago, April 24, 1965.

Proposed Standards for Membership in the Association

A. Educational Requirements:

Educational preparation for membership in the Association should contribute to the pastoral counselor's training and development a broad experience-related understanding of man-in-his-existence. It should take place in a setting in which the pastor can relate theoretical knowledge to, and derive it from, his pastoral work with people: i.e., a setting in which both the school and the practicum situation are in mutual relation.

1. It should give him:

   a. Familiarity with a wide variety of approaches to the conceptualization of personality, personality development, and interpersonal relationships, including the familial, phenomenological, social and cultural perspectives,
   b. Mastery of a coherent theory of personality and the counseling relationship which is useful in interpreting the intra- and inter-personal dynamics of counselees and the counseling process,
   c. Ability to use the language and methodology of differential diagnosis and to relate diagnosis to counseling

practice, including familiarity with the contributions of various diagnostic tests. (Ability to administer diagnostic tests is ordinarily not expected nor encouraged.)

d. Understanding of the dynamics of religious experience, and the implications for pastoral counseling.
e. Methods of research in counseling.
f. Ability to think theologically about the counseling task and the relation of counseling to the total task of the religious community.
g. Ability to relate the contributions of various disciplines to the counseling task in coherent and useful ways, and to make appropriate use of inter-professional collaboration to meet the needs of counselees.

2. The following areas of study are considered important for the achievement of the educational objectives:

 a. Theories of Personality and Personality Development
 b. Interpersonal Relations
 c. Marriage and Family Dynamics
 d. Group Dynamics
 e. Personality and Culture
 f. Psychopathology
 g. The Psychology of Religious Experience
 h. Theories of Counseling and Psychotherapy
 i. Theories of the Pastoral Office, including the history and theory of pastoral care
 j. Research Methods
 k. Orientation to the helping professions.

B. Requirements for Clinical Work under Supervision:

Clinical preparation for membership in the Association should contribute to the pastoral counselor's training and development of actual experience in counseling under the following kinds of supervision: Individual supervision, group supervision, supervision in intake and referral, supervision of marriage counseling, supervision in depth by at least two different supervisors, and interdisciplinary clinical case conference supervision.

For membership in each of the Divisions of the Association there is required a specified total number of hours of supervision. It is recommended that the percentage of time spent in the various kinds of supervision be as follows:

1. Twenty percent (20%) of the total time under individual supervision in depth. Units of supervision in depth are defined as twenty-five (25) consecutive supervisory hours with the same supervisor concerning the counseling with the same client.

2. Ten percent (10%) of the total time under supervision in intake and referral.

3. Thirty-five percent (35%) of the total time under continuous case supervision. This type of supervision is defined as a small group of pastoral counseling students in turn presenting clinical material from sessions with the same client for several consecutive supervisory conferences.

4. Thirty-five percent (35%) of the total time in clinical case conference. This type of supervision is usually interdisciplinary, including one or more representatives from the other helping professions: Psychiatrist, psychologist, and psychiatric social worker. It is recommended that a significant portion of supervision under this heading include a psychiatrist or other non-clergy professional trained in modern theories of psychodynamics.

C. Requirements for Personal Therapeutic Experience:

It is recommended for one Division and required for two Divisions of the Association that members shall have undergone sufficient personal psychotherapeutic investigation of his own intrapsychic processes that he is able to protect the counselee from his own problems, and to deploy himself to the maximum benefit of the counselee. It is also recommended that after April 30th, 1966 all candidates for membership in the Association have their qualifications reviewed in a face to face meeting with the Membership Committee. The Committee's task should include an examination of the candidates:

1. Personal Identity and Interpersonal Competence. It is the intent of this standard to ascertain the extent of the candidate's sense of his own selfhood, his awareness of his own internal dynamics, and the flexibility of his relatedness to others.
2. Academic and Theoretical Competence. It is the purpose of this standard to determine how well the candidate is able to correlate his knowledge of the behavioral sciences with his theological understanding, and to integrate theory and practice.
3. Therapeutic Competence. It is the intent of this standard to assess the candidate's awareness of his pastoral role, the relationship of his theological concepts to that role, his perspectives and his understanding of the doctrines of man, the church, and spiritual resources.
4. Ethical Commitment. It is the purpose of this standard to assess the candidate's understanding of and agreement with the Association's Code of Ethics for pastoral counseling, the degree of his awareness of the possibilities of exploiting the counselee, and the definition of his own personal and professional limits.[5]

When may the counselor say, "Now I am fully prepared"? Never can he stop preparing. To give up, even for a moment, the

[5] *American Association of Pastoral Counselors Manual,* 1965-66, pp. 18-20.

unfinished task of growing and the ongoing discipline of learning is to weaken and decline. There will be hours of recreation and days of rest, to be sure, for they are essential to the rhythm of growing life. But even so there is something to learn in each moment that will contribute to the growing that is to become a larger and deeper life. He will prepare before and after each interview, specifically; yet the learning will go on continuously in every moment of conversation, observation, self-examination, and prayer, without ceasing. He will be studying always: personality, diagnosis, principles of counseling, and a theology of mediating relationship. There will be tape recordings to make, interviews to write and case studies to evaluate by searching analysis. He will submit his work regularly to a supervisor, or a group of colleagues such as the staff of a counseling center, or a seminar of pastors and mental health consultants.

This he must do, not less but more. He must reconsider his responsibility, from hour to hour and person to person, toward those who come for counseling, or with whom he is related in the home, the church, and the community of man and God. He must continually be asking: "What shall I initiate and carry forward? When shall I wait for the other person to take the lead? No event or meeting is trivial or lacking in ultimate significance. How can I be responsible unless I am forever ready to learn, to search for meaning, and to perceive clearly my place and role in relation to each person I meet?"

3. *Ethical Concerns*

We live in a time of ethical confusion. There is no single standard of ethical conduct in a rapidly changing, plural society, where new ways make ancient good uncouth. What parents say to their children about right and wrong may not be very convincing to young people who want to decide for themselves. The moral authorities of the past were speaking to a different world. The preacher, the judge, and the policeman are standing for principles that may not be welcome or acceptable to the impetuous or the serious doubters who go their own way.

But there is a new ethical concern in our mid-century. Customs and mores that have continued for generations are now challenged as unworthy of human dignity. Declarations of human rights are extended to all people and written into laws and constitutions. Conscientious objection to war has become a crucial issue in a time of nuclear weapons. The right of self-determination is claimed in rising revolt against the rule of colonial powers. The inequalities of race are now the concern of all, as shown in legislation, court decisions, and freedom marches. The plight of the poor, the aged, and the sick awakens the public conscience to enact legislation and send workers to serve whatever person may be in need.

In a democratic society we say that every person has the right to decide what he will believe about moral, political, and religious questions. And we say that we ought to respect the beliefs of other persons even when they differ from our own. In this we honor the private judgment of the individual person to act from inner choice. Yet this is not unlimited freedom, for an individual is responsible to the laws and moral expectations of society for the sake of other persons whose rights are no less than his own.

The counselor has a public responsibility surrounding his private freedom. When he offers to serve other persons he must be ethically concerned for them. The American Psychological Association defines this responsibility in general principles emerging from specific incidents.

The worth of a profession is measured by its contribution to the welfare of man. Psychology seeks to further our knowledge of man and to better his condition by applying this knowledge to the solution of human problems. But a profession serves mankind only in an abstract sense; upon each individual psychologist rests the real responsibility for service. Whether a psychologist can properly fulfill this responsibility depends in part on his scientific and technical competence and in part on the values defining his relationships with other people. Values are personal, and each psychologist must work out his own value commitments. . . . Reflected in each principle of this code of ethics of psychologists is the fundamental belief that a psychologist will maintain an enduring concern for the effects of his professional acts on the lives of his fellow men.[6]

How will the counselor participate in the ethical concerns of persons who come to him? Will he influence and shape the ethical decisions of a client or take a neutral position? He will respect the right of the individual to decide, yet he will also be concerned for the values at stake and the outcome of the decisions. Where does the counselor's responsibility begin and end if his client is considering suicide or homicide, divorce or dishonesty?

A physician may treat bodily ills without inquiring about the moral or religious beliefs of the patient. He may see his responsibility to be that of healing the sick and relieving the misery of anyone who suffers, whatever his beliefs may be. But the psychotherapist deals with the emotional life where personal beliefs and values are of great concern. He is consulted about the problems of conduct and the practical relationships of daily life, where

[6] *Ethical Standards of Psychologists: A Summary of Ethical Principles* (American Psychological Association, 1333 Sixteenth Street, N.W., Washington, D.C., 1953), p. 1.

moral choices are central. How can he do the work of counseling apart from these moral concerns?

Psychologist Perry London shows how the very goals of psychotherapy are moral issues. What does the therapist want to happen in this person's life, and how does he hope to alter the life and goals of the person? This is a moral question that is always answered by the therapist in practice, even when it is not stated in words. As London says, "The very nature of his interaction with the people he serves involves a moral confrontation," in which he will surely communicate some part of his own moral commitments.

No one seriously doubts that this is true of the pastoral counselor for he is well known to stand for a moral and religious system. Other counselors may not acknowledge their moral commitment so openly; but it is there in every response, even when they intend to be neutral and withold moral judgment. The person comes for help to the counselor as one who is perceived to be an authority. Whatever the counselor says or does not say will have its influence upon the person. Otherwise, why invest the time in this relationship?

The notion that the psychotherapist's situation differs much from the priest's is, I believe, a convenient fiction. . . . To convince himself that he is not imposing his own value system upon his client —merely because he does not want to impose it—is ultimately to deceive both the client and himself. For this belief implicitly denies the essence of the psychotherapeutic relationship: that its most critical points are those involving the *interactions* between participants, not the private experiences of either of them. In other words, psychotherapy is a social, interpersonal action, characterized by an exchange of individual, personal ideas and feelings. The verbal content of the exchange differs with the respective roles of client and therapist, but the relationship is, in vital respects, a reciprocal one. The very fact of the exchange relationship dictates, I believe, the inevitability of the therapist's functioning practically as a moral agent.[7]

But how do I know what is best for you? I do not know enough to decide for you in the midst of your own unique experience. But I can bring you to see what it means to experience your predicament from the view of another person who cares for your potential being. We are both limited in our knowledge, but not at the same points. Each of us has some knowledge to contribute from his different awareness as he perceives the situation. Each has something to learn of the other and something to give to the other. I can search with you for the meaning of our encounter in this hour, and go with you in your life adventure for a stretch of the way.

Is it fair for me to impose my values on you? It is not fair to deceive or coerce you into believing as I do, against your better judgment. The aim of counseling is to remove pressure and go beyond deception to honest and open communication. I bring no ready-made solution, but some basic principles to try out as working hypotheses. We hope together to gain a larger perspective on this dilemma, with a guiding sense of what others have discovered along life's way. My task is not to impose but to propose a direction to explore, a path of light to follow step by step along the dark corridors of uncertainty. The values I hope to bring are exploratory but capable of growth through dialogue in our interviews. Whatever light we may find is not to be hidden

[7] Perry London, *The Modes and Morals of Psychotherapy* (New York: Holt, Rinehart and Winston, 1964), pp. 11-12.

in the dark of privacy, but shared in the light of open communication and searching examination.

Psychologist James Bugental expounds his approach to psychotherapy as a search for authenticity.[8] To be authentic is to be at one with the whole of being. This does not mean "adaptation" or "adjustment" to popular opinion to avoid conflict. The reference is to a more ultimate and ideal reality. The world of daily events is set in a larger world of authentic being, in which the meaning of human life is to be found. Authenticity does not call us to reject the familiar world or deny the values and activities of our associates. It is rather the awareness or perspective with which we participate in the events of our human lives.

We are bound to experience anxiety in our finite existence. We do not know enough to insure the outcome of our desires, which are subject to influences we cannot anticipate or control and to the losses of time and death. We have the potential to act, and so we discover we have responsibility. Yet we are subject to guilt when our choices miscarry, and to emptiness when we do not find the meaning of life. Though we are separate in the pangs of loneliness, we are related to other persons even amid our differences. Out of these anxieties we may try to escape into unreality. Neurosis is "the denial or distortion of authenticity. To the extent that we let fear or expediency pervert our perceptions of and responses to what is real in our lives, to that extent we are neurotic."[9]

What is real is our being thrown into a world we cannot well manage or comprehend. In our life transactions we seek certainty

[8] *The Search for Authenticity: An Existential-Analytic Approach to Psychotherapy* (New York: Holt, Rinehart and Winston, 1965.)
[9] *Ibid.*, p. 41.

where it does not exist, and disavow responsibility we cannot really avoid. When anxiety is unbearable, we constrict our world and ourselves to safe boundaries.

> Psychotherapy is not a healing process. It is a philosophic venture. It is not the treatment of an illness. It is daring to confront self-and-world. . . .
>
> The therapeutic relationship is not the agent of but the medium in which therapeutic change occurs. The agent is self-and-world confrontation. What makes possible the changes in the patient's being-in-the-world is his discarding of some of the constrictions he has put on himself-and-his-world sufficiently to recognize their limiting and hurtful effects. With such recognition, the patient may choose less destructive ways of being-in-the-world, with a resulting increase in authenticity. In order to discard these constrictions the patient must experience the anxiety (whether neurotic or existential) the constrictions were erected to dispel. Generally, this is insupportable, unless there is some other way of sustaining himself in the world during the transition. This the therapeutic relationship can often provide.[10]

There are three moving actions in the search for authenticity. (1) I seek to be as fully aware as I can be at the moment. (2) I choose how I will invest my life. (3) I take responsibility for the choice I have made, whatever may come, whether tragic suffering or joy, from my actions and my limitations.[11]

This much and more will be involved in a sound ethical decision. A person will look within himself to be aware of his dynamic inner experience. But he will also look beyond himself

[10] *Ibid.*, p. 42.

[11] *Ibid.*, p. 45. The value of responsibility as a therapeutic agent is also the theme of William Glasser in *Reality Therapy* (New York: Harper & Row, 1965).

to measure his desire against the larger reality to which he is responsible. For no person can be authentic in himself alone but always in relation to Thou. To be in the world one must respond to that which is beyond himself. To be wholly there is to participate in an act of transcendence. Otherwise he is encapsulated within the illusions of a self-limiting, fragmentary existence.

The struggle to be independent is a heroic quest for personal identity. This is one goal, but not the ultimate goal of the human adventure. Not until a person transcends himself does he truly find himself as a whole person. We may say it is childish to be dependent, yet there is a wisdom of childhood we dare not lose. Life is fulfilled through relationships in which we depend upon one another in mutual interdependence. In a larger sense we depend upon the whole cosmos for life and the Ultimate Being for the meaning of our being.

4. The Central Focus

The most decisive determinant in human life is the central focus. The focus of attention changes from moment to moment as we turn from one item to another in the day's work or in driving along the street. Yet there is a central purpose that unifies all the details of the day's work, and a destination to guide the course of our progress from street to street. A focus is the point of vision at which all rays converge. Until the eyes focus the field is blurred, but when the focus is precise the vision is sharp and clear. Yet the act of focusing is more than adjusting the eye muscles; it involves the whole range of intricate responses which a person makes to the cumulative stimuli pressing upon him. The central focus of a person's life is the meeting and integrating of all inner and outer relationships.

Is human behavior inner-directed or outer-directed? Personalists like William James and Gordon Allport, perceptual psychologists like Donald Snygg and Carl Rogers, existentialists like Viktor Frankl and Ludwig Binswanger, see our lives directed by inner experience. Physical, social, and economic determinists, as well as many stimulus-response psychologists, see life as outer-directed by forces impinging upon and controlling the individual person. Sigmund Freud traces the conflicting forces within the individual's conscious-unconscious life in response to the persons who are most significant to him.

Each observer of human behavior has his central focus from which he views every act and motive. He can see how decisive this central focus is for the theory which flows into it and the practice which emerges from it. He will show how life is determined in one way or another; he may avow his belief in a complete determinism. Yet he exercised freedom to choose the central focus of his determinism. And he reasons with us to present the claims of his theory against others, in confident expectation that we are free to choose what we believe, and decide what is true and false.

The central focus of our responsive counseling is *mediation.*[12] Human behavior, from this viewpoint, is a dynamic interaction between converging stimuli and intentional responses. The inner life is determined somewhat, but not finally, by the outer world. The inner life is neither helpless nor omnipotent. Fulfillment of the inner life does not come by withdrawal from or defense against the outer world, but in open and continuous

[12] This we have seen in Chapter 2 from a theological perspective. Here we see mediation as the central focus of ethical responsibility.

transactions with the world. Whoever and whatever comes to meet us is that to which we respond as each of us chooses from moment to moment, among the alternatives open to him.

To mediate is to be in the middle of interacting forces and persons, seeking to reconcile and unify them. Each person is a middleman between other persons and events in his world. He is never really alone, even though he may feel lonely and deserted or isolated and resistant to the life around him. His ongoing life is continually under the confluence of inner and outer pressures, which are frequently conflicting or confusing. Yet he is always seeking to relate the welter of fragments into meaningful wholes. Out of these frustrations, anxieties, hostilities, uncertainties, and contrasting desires he may come to a counselor to resolve the traffic jam. He is hoping that a counselor will help him to work through his blockade into more open communication. And if the counseling proceeds well, he will hope to work out his transactions among the significant persons and events of his many-sided existence.

The responsive counselor aims to be a mediator in these complex and often tangled interactions and interrelationships. The counselor in marital and family counseling will not take sides with one against the other. He will not be pushing or pulling from one side to the other, or throwing his weight around to tip the scales in favor of this person or that decision, but standing between these persons in their search for fulfillment in a more creative relationship. He will be listening to each one and seeing the opposing forces and points of view, while accepting each person in his stage of potential growth. He will be mediating the conflicts, separations, and fragmentations into the integrity of interrelating wholeness. He will seek to mediate the proximate with the ultimate concerns of man and God in the revealing address and response of "I and Thou."

As the counselor mediates for the person among persons, he will see the counselee as a potential mediator, who is already and always engaging in transactions with other persons. Yet at this moment of his life history, he is needing to learn and asking to grow more effectually into the true mediator he seeks to become. If he is to be a mediator he must learn to accept the unacceptable, to bear the stress of the involving relationship, and to call forth the hidden best from another person. So the counselor is at work to awaken the mediating potential of this person.

The pastor in all his dimensions and within his expanding limitations seeks to be such a mediator. He invites the Creative Spirit to infuse and transfuse his being with a greater and self-giving agape love. He offers to take upon his heart the emotional burdens of others, the conflicting, anguishing distresses of fear, hostility, or guilt; and to bear them with the person as a means of grace and growth. He aims to participate in such counseling as will help to relate estranged persons and fragmentary lives into reconciling love and trusting acceptance, to forgive the unforgiving, to offer a more creative life to the uncreative, to release into freedom the person in bondage, that new life may stir and begin to grow.

He knows the answers are not really his own, that the power to grow is not from himself alone, but from his vital and mutual relationship to "Thou," from whom is streaming, as from the sun, replenishing light and warmth for all to share. His usefulness as a counselor requires humility not to claim or dispense authority in arbitrary ways. Yet he is not to hide or efface himself, but to give himself fully to be a mediator to and with other persons. His authority is mediated to him through the living community of sustaining and reviving relationships, where he is known and trusted to serve other persons in responsible mediation. Relying, as he must, upon the community of all these religious-social-educative-therapeutic relationships, he seeks no arbitrary authority but rather mutual consent, and response of the ultimate Thou and the many "thous" with whom he holds this uncommon life in common. The counselor is called to arbitrate in the midst of conflict, to reconcile in the enmities of estrangement, and to act ever faithfully among the transactions of persons seeking to grow in the spirit of creative love.

Index